CHA KIMOON
JOURNEY for THE ETERNAL LIFE

Autobiographical Essay

JOURNEY for THE ETERNAL LIFE
Copyright ⓒ 2025 by Cha Kimoon All rights reserved

English version First Edition Published August 4, 2025

Published by Geulnurim Publishing co.
MoonChang B/D F2, 6-6, Donggwang-ro 46-gil, Seocho-gu, Seoul, Korea

Author by Cha Kimoon
Publisher by Jongsook Choi

Includes index.
ISBN 978-89-6327-763-9 03810
Registration 303-2005-000038(Date 5th October 2005)

e-mail: geulnurim2005@daum.net
TEL 02-3409-2055 | FAX 02-3409-2059

정가 35,000원(U.S. $25)

Printed in South Korea.

JOURNEY for THE ETERNAL LIFE
CHA KIMOON

Autobiographical Essay

Writer **Cha Kimoon**

- Korean Military Academy (23rd Class)
- U.S. Army Command & General Staff College (1978 Class)
- Korea University (MBA)
- U.S. Troy State University (MBA)
- Kyeungnam University (Ph.D)
- Operational Staff of the 6th Corps (G3)
- Chief of Staff of the 5th Corps
- Commander of the 37th Infantry Division
- Presidential Secretary of Defense (Blue House)
- DCS of the ROK/US Combined Forces Command & Senior Member of the UNC Military Armistice Commission
- Retired Lieutenant General (Army)
- Professor, Cheongju University
- Professor, Pyeongtaek University
- Director, International Education Center
- Chairman of the ROK/U.S. Forum

Autonym

- From the Armistice to Peace
- Righteous War
- and others

Preface

Generally, a written account of one's life is called an autobiography. When the focus shifts more toward the environment or era in which the author lived, it becomes a memoir. Some autobiographies, such as Goethe's Poetry and Truth, weave in creative elements and have literary value. This book is neither a heroic memoir in the vein of Churchill, MacArthur, or Schweitzer nor a literary work of the caliber of Tolstoy or Goethe.

Rather, it is a raw, essay-style expression of the inner record of my life. Its purpose is to pass on my experiential philosophy of life as an inspiration for future generations. Only when one is prepared to cast aside this single life like a blade of grass for the sake of the nation and humanity, one can attain eternal life. Life becomes eternal not through the pursuit of personal gain or comfort but through a resolute view of life and death—one devoted to defending the nation and striving for world peace.

I came of age in a generation marked by turmoil. Born in the final years of World War II, during the final throes of Japanese imperialism, I lived through the Korean War. Amid the painful division of my homeland, I witnessed the righteous struggle to defend democracy. My worldview was deeply shaped by the crimson blood of the 4.19 Student Revolution, a movement that rose against one-party dictatorship and was marked by the sacrifice of many lives. I entered the Korea Military Academy in the aftermath of the 5.16 Military Coup, which was driven by the goal of national modernization. Our generation lived through the assassination of Park Chung Hee on October 26 and the military insurrection on December 12 and, ultimately, the 6.10 Struggle, which brought forth the flower of democratization. Many of us went on to lead the IT industry, spearheading the information age and becoming pioneers in the era of artificial intelligence. Even amid such upheaval, we were the generation that transformed a once-primitive society into a highly advanced civilization in just a few decades—building on 5,000 years of history. We were key figures in the proud emergence of a modern nation, having brought about industrialization, democratization, informatization, and the AI era while overcoming the shame of once being called a backward country.

I was born and raised in remote mountain village by the Nakdong River during an era of widespread poverty. People survived by eating roots and tree bark, but I went to Daegu to pursue my education as a boy passionate about learning. From an early age, I learned to live independently, away from my parents and developed a strong sense of self-reliance while dedicating myself to my studies. Thanks to scholarships from various foundations, including the Rotary and Lions Clubs, I was able to rise from nothing. No matter how difficult the circumstances, I fully benefited from the opportunities in my homeland, where anyone could freely develop their innate talents.

I wanted to honorably repay the grace given to me by my country and society, so I chose the path of self-sacrifice and dedication to public service. I entered the Korea Military Academy. The life of a soldier is not one of ease, driven by personal interests; rather, it is a challenging and righteous path in which one sacrifices their life for a greater cause. I devoted myself to the nation, the people, and world peace, seeking eternal life through faith in God and a life of service.

I began keeping a journal in elementary school. Although there have been inevitable interruptions along the way, my record will continue until the day I take my last breath. This book is based on the stories from my journals. The notes and essays

I've written over the years, along with the photographs stored in albums, USB drives, and PC files, have all helped bring memories back to life.

This book is divided into two parts. Part I describes my dreams of ambition. While gazing at the tranquil flow of the Nakdong River along Deoksilgol, a remote mountain village, I pondered what I should do for the country, the people, and humanity and left my hometown. With an indomitable will, I dedicated myself to my studies, adopting the spirit of the great principles as my motto: "Love others and never deceive myself." I entered Hwarangdae and tempered myself in the furnace of life, striving to realize my lofty dreams.

Part 2 vividly portrays my life as a soldier, from my time as a junior officer to a general. It recounts my experiences, including searching for armed North Korean infiltrators in the Seoraksan region, navigating life-and-death moments in the jungles of Vietnam war under the Cross of the Southern Star, and later serving as the Defense Secretary of President at the Blue House, Deputy Chief of Staff at the ROK-U.S. Combined Forces Command, and Senior Membrer of the Military Armistice Commission. In these roles, I played a key part in developing and implementing national strategies and policies.

My life has been guided by the belief: 'Take action, and opportunities will open up,' and 'Without obsessive passion, there is no greatness.' I approached my work with unwavering loyalty and a deep sense of mission, dedicating myself to the nation, the people, and world peace. With the remaining passion, I devoted myself to mentoring the next generation.

I owe my deepest gratitude to my wife, Kim Kyeung-ah; daughter, Cha Soo-jin; son-in-law, Kim Ju-hyeuk; son, Cha Jeong-seok; and daughter-in-law, Park Bok-seon, for their help in collecting materials and proofreading this book. Hoping that this work may serve as a guiding light for young people pursuing an immortal life, I dedicate this work to the souls of those who gave their lives for the country and the people.

Cha Kimoon

August 2025
Songpa, Seoul

Contents

Preface ... 5

| Part I | The Pursuit of Lofty Dreams

Chapter 1 Childhood in Deoksilgol

    1. Born as a Farmer's Son in Deoksilgol ... 17
    2. 41st Generation of the *Yeonan Cha* Clan ... 22
    3. My Father's Lesson, "Stay Resolute in All Things" ... 28
    4. My Mother, the Embodiment of Affection and Love ... 37
    5. Childhood Friends Who Shared Everything Down to the Last Candy ... 47
    6. Outbreak of the Korean War and My Childhood ... 54
    7. Six Years of Excellence and Perfect Attendance at Deokgok Elementary School ... 77

Chapter 2 My Youth Away from Home

    1. From Deoksilgol to Daegu ... 89
    2. The Rising Star by Suseong Stream ... 95
    3. Junk Boots from the Yankee Market ... 105
    4. Years of Turmoil ... 111
    5. The Spirit of Martial Arts Cultivated in the Judo Hall ... 116

Chapter 3   The Immortal Spirit of the Hwarang

    1. My First Step into the Hwarangdae   123
    2. Human Transformation: Basic Military Training   132
    3. In the Crucible of Life   141
    4. Army, Navy, and Air Force Cadets' Brotherhood Oath   151
    5. Daily Test System   158
    6. The Heart-Throbbing Hwarang Festival   166
    7. The Star of Hwarangdae   171

| Part II | Guardians of the Nation

Chapter 1   The Years as a Company Officer

    1. Officer Basic Course at the Infantry School   181
    2. Three Musketeers to the 17th Regiment   185
    3. Vietnamese Language Training School   199
    4. To the Vietnam war   206
    5. The ROK/US Combined Planning Staff   220
    6. Public Proposal and Marriage   223
    7. Being a Company Commander and Newlywed   233
    8. The Tearful Farewell Ceremony of the Company Commander   241
    9. To the Officer Advanced Course   246

Chapter 2   The Years as a Field Officer

    1. The Cradle of Military Education: ROK Army College   257
    2. Operations Officer of the ROK/US Combined 1st Corps and the 8.18 Hatchet Massacre   263
    3. Studying at the U.S. Army Command and General Staff College   270
    4. Wargame Officer and Promotion to Lieutenant Colonel   283

5. Airborne Training During Leave	287
6. Commander of the 9th Division's Reconnaissance Battalion	294
7. The Military Faction Scandal	301
8. Designated to the Samcheong Education Center	307
9. The Best Regiment in the RCT	312
10. Vanguard Regiment in the Team Spirit Exercise	320
11. Selected as the Operations Officer of the 6th Corps	328

Chapter 3   **The Years as a General**

1. Chief of Staff of the 5th Corps	337
2. Serving at Coast Guard Posts on the East, West, and South Coasts	346
3. My Connection with the 37th Division	353
4. Defense Secretary to the Blue House	373
5. DCS of the ROK/US Combined Forces Command & Senior Member of the Military Armistice Commission	381
6. Departing from Active Duty	398

Epilogue   411

The Ten Commandments of Leadership

Part I

The Pursuit of Lofty Dreams

Chapter 1

•

| Childhood in Deoksilgol |

1. Born as a Farmer's Son in Deoksilgol

Deoksilgol, my hometown where the Nakdong River winds its way! After a two-hour ride from Daegu on an unpaved road, the bus finally reaches Bammari Ferry on the riverbank. After I board the ferry by the shore, the boatman rows across the current, and on the opposite bank, my mother greets me with joy. There was no fixed fare for the ferry. One did not pay cash each time. Instead, ferry tolls are paid in grain—18 liters of barley in summer and 18 liters of rice in autumn, twice a year. Whether you took the ferry ten times or a hundred, the fare was always settled with harvested grain.

The Deoksilgol Bammari Ferry is located where the headwaters of the Nakdong River meet another tributary, the Hoecheon Stream, creating a favorable site for a port due to the deep water. Thanks to these natural conditions, a large five-day market was held, becoming a hub for various goods exchanges. The five-day markets included Bammari, Ibang, Guji, Hyeonpung, Chogye, and Goryeong Market.

Five-day market   Ogwangdae Mask Play

All of these five-day markets developed around the Nakdong River. In particular, Bammari Market was one of the most prosperous five-day markets during the Joseon Dynasty. During that time, the Bammari Ferry became a central transportation hub for people and goods along the Nakdong River, also serving as a lively riverside port where many carefree wanderers passed through.

On market days, not only did people gather to buy and sell goods, but performers from all across the region also assembled.

There were farmers' traditional music performances, wrestling contests, and Ogwangdae Mask Plays that flourished alongside them. The origin of Ogwangdae Mask Play can be traced back to my hometown, Bammari. Long ago, a coachman called "Malttugi" lived beyond the mountains in Chogye. His surname was Park, and he was originally of noble birth, but he lived as a servant. In Deoksilgol, the aristocrats were harsh and looked down upon or belittled commoners and servants. In anger, Malttugi learned of the private affairs of the aristocrats and exposed their misdeeds in front of a gathering of about ten villagers. From then on, whenever Malttugi showed his face, he was met with disdain from the aristocrats, so he began wearing a mask. This is said to be the origin of the Bammari Ogwangdae Mask Play.

If you travel about 4 kilometers inland along the rural road from Bammari on the Nakdong River, you will reach a beautiful, secluded mountain village where peach blossoms are in full bloom, farmers leisurely herd their cattle, and skylarks sing. This is the very place where I was born and raised—Deoksilgol. Now, with a bridge built over the Nakdong River and well-maintained paved roads, Deoksilgol has transformed into a suburban area just 30 minutes away from Daegu.

Deoksilgol

However, until the 1960s, Deoksilgol was a quiet and peaceful mountain village. Danamsan (378m) stands to the south, and Sohaksan (489m) gently rises to the north, making it a place of unrivaled beauty. In spring, the azaleas on the front mountain would turn red, painting the entire landscape with vibrant hues like a picture. In summer, mischievous children splashing in the stream added to the peaceful charm. When autumn arrived, the golden fields of ripened grain would sway in the wind, and farmers would gaze happily at the sparrows flying away in surprise at the dancing scarecrows. In winter, Deoksilgol was where people gathered around the fireplace, sharing stories of old times.

Although Deoksilgol was renamed Deokgok-myeon, it

had long been a village known for its kindness and generosity, often referred to as *Deoksildaeck* (a term for a newlywed woman moving to another village). It is located in Hapcheon County, Gyeongsangnam-do. However, due to its proximity to Daegu, most people commute to Daegu to study, do business, and visit relatives. When Busan, the provincial capital of Gyeongsangnam-do, was a major hub, the Nakdong River served as the main transportation route, and there was much interaction. However, with the shift to land-based transportation, people now prefer Daegu, which is geographically closer to Busan. While my older siblings studied in Busan, I, the youngest, attended school in Daegu, a change brought about by the shift in transportation.

I was born on August 4, 1944 (the 17th day of the 4th lunar month) as the fifth of six siblings to Chae Gyeong-bong and Jeon Sun-seon, farmers in Deoksilgol. This was a time when the remnants of Japanese imperialism forced us to stop speaking our language and writing our characters, and we were made to learn Japanese and sing Japanese songs from elementary school.

Because it was the final stage of the Pacific War, imperialist Japan was making its last desperate efforts. Men were not allowed to seek employment freely.

The era of Japanese imperialism

A regulation was created to forcibly enlist students, turning young, promising individuals into cannon fodder on the battlefield. A group called the "Women's Volunteer Corps" was formed, and unmarried women were taken to the front lines, where they were exploited as sexual prey by the imperial army.

2. 41st Generation of the *Yeonan Cha* Clan

I am the 41st generation descendant of the *Yeonan Cha* clan, born in the leap-fourth month of the lunar calendar. Deoksilgol, a village formed by members of the Cha clan, celebrated family events like birthdays as if one large family shared them. Since I was born in a leap month, a rare occurrence in the lunar calendar, it was difficult to celebrate my birthday more than two or three times in a lifetime. For that reason, unlike most people of my generation, I observe my birthday according to the solar calendar. The 17th day of the leap, the fourth lunar month, translates to June 7 in the solar calendar. However, at the time, administrative systems in rural areas were not well organized, and my father asked a neighbor heading to the distant township office to register my birth. The neighbor misremembered the date and mistakenly entered August 4, 1944, on my family registry. Although it was an error, I now observe August 4 as my official birthday. Even Jesus's registered birthday and actual birth are different—yet December 25, the date on the official record, is celebrated as Christmas. In the same way, rather than waiting for a birthday that comes around only three times in a lifetime, I simply celebrate the solar calendar date, August 4, that everyone already recognizes as my birthday.

My father and mother originally had eight children—five sons and three daughters. However, the two brothers just above me, whose names I never came to know, died young from measles in infancy, so in effect, we were six siblings: Cha Jeong-bun (daughter), Cha Jeong-geum (daughter), Cha Ki-whan (son), Cha Ki-hong (son), Cha Kimoon (son), and Cha Jeong-sook (daughter).

Because the two older brothers I never met were gone, there was a considerable age gap between me and what was effectively my second eldest brother, Cha Ki-hong. Being much older, he became my mentor. Even before I entered elementary school, he was a strict instructor who taught me Hangul and multiplication tables with a switch in hand. My second eldest brother did not hide his dissatisfaction with our parents. In Korea, where Confucianism runs deep, parents placed great importance on the eldest son since ancestral rites were passed down through him.

My second eldest brother used to complain about our parents' tendency to prioritize the eldest brother in everything. Clothes were always bought with the eldest brother in mind, shoes were chosen for him first, and he was given priority in education, naturally leaving the second eldest brother dissatisfied. Nevertheless, the bond between our siblings was unusually strong. During family ceremonies or holidays, the entire family would gather at the eldest brother's house to spend joyful times together.

My youngest sister, Cha Jeong-sook, and I shared many stories and memories from an early age. Being three years apart, we naturally spent much time growing close. We would lie on either side of our mother, each holding onto one of her breasts, pestering her to turn and face our side. We shared dried persimmons by her side and drifted off to sleep with our heads on her arms while listening to lullabies. In the summer, my mother would light mosquito coils and sit with us on the wooden floor, roasting corn and telling us old stories. We sometimes put potatoes in the rice pot and, once cooked, argue over who would get more.

Deoksilgol is a clan village where members of the Cha family have settled in a tight-knit community. The Cha family was a distinguished noble lineage that produced 25 ministers during the Silla period.

However, during the reign of King Ae-jang of Silla, a man named Eon-seung, who was the king's uncle, assassinated the king and seized the throne for himself, becoming King Heon-deok. Cha Seung-saek, a descendant of Cha Mu-il—the founder of the Cha family and once favored by King Ae-jang—attempted to eliminate Eon-seung, but his plan was exposed in advance, and he fled to Mt. Guwolsan in Yeonan, Hwanghae Province. In order to avoid detection by Eon-seung, now King Heon-deok, Cha Seung-saek adopted the surname Ryu, which shared the same meaning as his grandmother's surname Yang, thus assuming a false identity as Ryu Seung-saek.

Family Tree

Cha Kyeung-bong — Jeon Soon-seun

1st son: Cha Ki-whan — Park Jeom-seon

Cha Seong-sook—Do Young-chan ➡ Do Wha-soo, Do Kyung-woo
Cha Seong-yeong—Park Jong-hoe ➡ Park Jin-hee, Park Jin-woo
Cha Seong-ja—Kim Ik-soo ➡ Kim Ji-eon, Kim Hyun-jae
Cha Won-seok
Cha Moon-seok—Son Ja-young
Cha Seong-hee—Son Young-joo ➡ Son Min-jae

2nd son: Cha Ki-hong — Baek Eun-sook

Cha Seok-jin—Park Kyung-soon ➡ Cha Il-dong, Cha Hyun-jung
Cha Chang-hyeon
Cha Joo-hyeon

3rd son: Cha Kimoon — Kim Kyeong-ah

Cha Soo-jin—Kim Joo-hyeuk
Cha Jeong-seok—Park Bok-seon ➡ Cha Min-seo, Cha Min-woo

1st daughter: Cha Jeong-bun — Park Joong-sik

Park Nak-jin-Shin Dong-sook ➡ Park Ok-hee
Park Seung-jin-Seo Bun—seon ➡ Park Ki-nam, Park Ki-man

2nd daughter: Cha Jeong-sook — Kim Kong-hee

Kim Ki-chaeon—Lee Yu-seon ➡ Kim Sun-mee, Kim Jong-heon
Kim Chun-ok—Kim Chan-il ➡ Kim So-young, Kim Bok-goo, Kim Min-jeong
Kim Young-ok—Kwon Cheo-gyu ➡ Kwon Sae-yong, Kwon Jin-mo
Kim Ki-bo—Song Hyang-sook ➡ Kim Chae-hyun, Kim jong-wan
Kim Ki–yong—Kim Yong-mee ➡ Kim Eeon-hae, Kim Jong-wook, Kim Jong-hyun

3rd daughter: Cha Jeong-sook — Cho Chang-rae

Cho Hye- kyeung—Kim Chang-sik ➡ Kim Chae-yeon, Kim Si-yeon
Cho Eeon—yong—Lee Ho-hyeung ➡ Lee Jeong-hyeok, Lee soo-rim
Cho Hyeun-il—Hong Seung-jeung ➡ Cho Jae–yong, Cho Jae-min

Cha family shrine in Uideoksa

From then on, the Cha family used the false surname Ryu until it was restored by King Taejo of Goryeo. Ryu Cha-dal, the sixth-generation descendant of Ryu Seung-saek, made significant contributions to the founding of the Goryeo Dynasty. In recognition, King Taejo awarded him a high government post and also restored the Cha surname to his eldest son, Ryu Hyo-jeon, who was living in Yeonan, Hwanghae Province, allowing him to be called Cha Hyo-jeon.

The descendants of Cha Hyo-jeon, who restored the Cha surname from the Ryu family, prospered greatly and eventually settled in the Nakdong River basin. This became the foundation, and those with the Cha surname now form most of Deoksilgol's population. The Cha family, which has lived in Deoksilgol for many years and formed a clan society, considers everyone—

whether older brother, older sister, uncle, or aunt—to be a relative, creating a sense of closeness and unity. When tracing the family lineage, I am the 41st generation descendant of the *Yeonan Cha* family, from the *Gang Yeolgong* branch.

3. My Father's Lesson, "Stay Resolute in All Things"

My father, Cha Kyeung-bong, the eldest son of the Cha family, inherited the family bloodline. He was born on September 23, 1910, the same year Japan annexed Korea, as the only son of my grandfather, Cha Su-hyeong. Since my grandmother had given birth to four daughters before finally having a son, my father was raised as an only son, cherished and adored. Born as a precious son, he grew up receiving the love of those around him, which made him somewhat self-centered and stubborn. However, he also had a strong sense of leadership and disliked losing to others. Having studied Confucianism, my father was deeply committed to Confucian values, and he ruled over our family and servants with a stern demeanor without ever getting his hands dirty. His commanding voice and gaze made him a strict head of the family.

My father was the village head, who took the lead whenever something happened in the village and earned the respect and admiration of many. The people of Deoksilgol were primarily engaged in farming. At that time, more than 80% of the population in our country worked in agriculture, and my father also farmed. Our family was relatively well-off in the village, as we employed two hired hands to help with the farming. While the entire village had thatched-roof houses, our house was the only one with a tiled roof. Sparrows built their nests on the edges of the thatched roofs. Whenever the village children boasted about finding bird eggs on their roofs, I couldn't help but feel a little envious of the thatched houses.

My father, Cha Kyeung-bong
(1910~1982)

My father, the only son, had many older sisters, but the ones closest to our family were my youngest aunt, who lived in the neighboring village of Yangchon, and my eldest aunt, who lived over the mountain in Yul-gok. Whenever my aunts' families visited, it felt like a festive occasion. We would slaughter chickens, and the carefully preserved dried mackerel would be served at the table. My house's flower garden was always full of various flowers, such as balsam, moss rose, and dandelions, blooming year-round. Among my cousins, my fourth cousins, Ok-seon and Bun-seon, were especially close to me. Playing hide-and-seek in the flower garden and teasing my cousins by lifting their skirts were the most enjoyable times.

Orchard hut

My aunt's house in Yul-gok was located by the Hwang River, so she grew many watermelons and melons. I often visited her house, enjoying the delight of breaking open watermelons while listening to the sounds of cicadas and watching the gently flowing river from the pavilion. My aunt was very kind-hearted, and whenever we visited, she would offer all kinds of food she had kept, such as fruits, taffy, and sweet rice drinks. This love and warm affection played a significant role in forming my healthy character.

My father's motto was "Stay Resolute in All Things," and he emphasized to his children, urging us to do everything perfectly. As the Bible says, "He who is faithful in small things will be faithful in great things," he always insisted that we give our best in even the smallest tasks. It is said that even a tiger uses all its strength to catch a rabbit. The family motto, "Stay Resolute in All Things," taught me to handle even the smallest tasks flawlessly, which later became a significant guiding principle in my life.

My father's dedication to the education of his children was stronger than anyone else's. It wasn't common for children in rural areas to be sent to cities for schooling, but my siblings and I had the opportunity to study in Busan and Daegu. In order to cover the tuition fees, my father sold cows and pigs, and when that wasn't enough, he even sold rice fields and farmland to continue our education. Since my father was an only son, my grandparents were adamantly opposed to their son leaving the house. Many people then went to Manchuria or Japan to study and broaden their horizons abroad. My father must have greatly envied them. He wanted to give his children the experiences of the wider world that he couldn't have, so he sent us to Busan and Daegu to pursue our education.

A working ox was essential to farm the land. In an era when farming tools were not yet developed, oxen handled most of the agricultural labor, so every household had at least one. Our family had a yellow working ox, and I was responsible for taking care of it. Since my older brothers left home to study right after graduating from elementary school, I, the youngest, was the only one left at home.

"Yoon-gil! Get up and boil the ox feed!!"

"Yes, Father!"

My childhood name was Yoon-gil. It was given to me by my eldest sister because I was born in a leap month, known as *Yoon-dal* in Korean. Even when it was still dark outside, my father, who was always an early riser, would loudly wake me—who loved to sleep in. But I never complained and jumped up at his call, heading straight to the cauldron in the detached quarters to boil the ox feed, breaking off pine branches to start the fire.

Nureong-i (yellow working ox)

When I lit the fire under the tightly frozen hearth and boiled the feed in the cauldron before giving it to the ox, it would grow noticeably day by day. With its bell clinking as it worked the fields, the yellow ox, *Nureong-i*, also gave birth to healthy calves.

The firewood used to boil the ox feed also served as the main source of heat for the men's quarters, kown as *sarangbang* in Korean, where the village elders gathered. It was also my job to prepare the brazier so the guests could smoke and to fetch a large basin of water for them to drink whenever they were thirsty. Because of these diligent acts, the villagers were full of praise for me.

When the day's farm work was done and evening came, villagers would gather one by one in the men's quarters of our house. The men's quarters served as a communal rest area and an open discussion space where anyone could come and go freely. Centered around my father, it became a forum for debating the village's development and prosperity. In the winter, they would catch roe deer and rabbits from the snow-covered mountains and cook them together. On the wallpaper of the men's quarters, there were dark marks behind the spots where people sat—stains left over many years from villagers leaning their heads against the wall.

When there was a celebration at any house in the village, a pig would be slaughtered. On big feast days, a cow would sometimes be slaughtered as well. At times, the villagers would gather together, agreeing to share the meat from each household and collecting money in advance to slaughter a cow or pig. This was also the occasion to prepare the meal for the men's quarters. The taste of freshly slaughtered meat, cooked right away without being frozen, was the true flavor of meat. Those who had never tasted freshly slaughtered beef or pork would never know that taste.

My father, who opened the men's quarters to create a village discussion room and took the lead in taking on the village's tough tasks, was widely known as a leader with strong leadership and exemplary character. He was highly respected and admired by the villagers as he served as the village head for many years due to their invitation. After I graduated from Deokgok Elementary School and left for Daegu to study, my father carried rice on his back and took me to Daegu. When he left me there to live independently, it seemed to bring a tear to his eye, though he tried to hide it. This tender side of him revealed that he was not just a strict village head but a father full of love and affection.

My father, who was especially affectionate toward me as the youngest, passed away at the age of 73 from old age at our family home. It has been a lifelong regret that I couldn't be by his side at his passing due to my military duties. He passed away on June 10, 1982 (according to the lunar calendar) while I was abroad on duty.

My father Cha Kyeung-bong's funeral

I received the news of my father's passing while I was on a business tour of Japan, the Philippines, Thailand, Indonesia, Singapore, Hong Kong, and Malaysia with General Kang Young-sik while working at the Joint Chiefs of Staff. At that time, communication with Southeast Asia was not well established, and flights to Korea were not easily available, so it took time for me to return. Even on the fastest flight, it was impossible to attend the funeral within three days. My eldest brother, Cha Ki-whan, insisted that the funeral could only proceed once I arrived, so he waited for me. As a result, we held a five-day funeral.

It was the sweltering heat of summer, and the entire family was drenched in sweat. The house, located in a rural area without refrigeration, was filled with an awful smell. However, upon returning from overseas, I embraced my father's body, crying all night long, begging for forgiveness as an ungrateful child. When I regained my composure with swollen eyes, my eldest brother, Cha Ki-whan, gently patted my shoulder and told me that Father had asked for me often during his last moments. While I had bought the bag Father wanted during my overseas trip, I was unable to give it to him. Father had always liked Choco Pies. I had hoped to see him enjoy the Choco Pies I brought.

4. My Mother,
the Embodiment of Affection and Love

My mother, Jeon Soon-seun, who was older than my father, was born on December 10, 1908, as the youngest daughter in a noble family of six daughters and one son in Jeongdong Village, beyond the mountain. Raised under the guidance of her maternal grandfather, studying Confucian texts, she grew up in a refined manner. At the age of 16, she married my father, who was two years younger than her. It was customary then for women to marry men younger than them, so my mother was older than my father. Although he was a young, childlike groom, my mother never retorted when my father raised his voice. Instead, she would wait patiently in the kitchen until his anger subsided. When they disagreed, my mother would not argue back but instead endured everything in silence. Once my father's anger had passed, she would then point out his mistakes, making her a typical Eastern woman, and their disagreements were never visible as fights.

My mother's affection for others was exceptionally deep. She would prepare abundant meals for the farmhands working in the fields, ensuring their bowls were piled high with rice so they wouldn't go hungry. When it was time for a snack, she prepared special dishes and took them to the fields. Whenever my mother would carry the basket of food on her head and head toward the fields, my younger sister, Jeong-sook, and I would follow her. I would carry the kettle, and my sister would carry the water bottle, happily splashing in the water as we walked along the rice field paths behind her.

As a child, it was incredibly joyful and exciting to hold my mother's hand and go to my maternal grandparents' house. The path over a small mountain to their house was beautiful every season: in spring, the azaleas bloomed in full, and in summer, the sound of cicadas filled the air. In autumn, fallen chestnuts and acorns would stop my steps, and in winter, the snow-covered trail added a serene beauty to the surroundings. I could pick and enjoy the ripe persimmons hanging from the persimmon tree in my grandparents' backyard, and I will never forget the taste of the sweet rice drink my grandmother made herself. I spent countless hours playing with my cousins by the stream, washing our faces and catching carp and catfish to make spicy fish stew. In autumn, we would catch grasshoppers in the fields, and when we gathered a full trap of loaches, my grandmother would cook a delicious loach soup. The taste of that naturally sourced loach soup is something I will never forget.

My Mother Jeon Soon-seun (1908~2000)

Our family was the head family, so many people would gather at our house during rituals and holidays. My mother would prepare an abundance of food and share it with the villagers. When those who came to eat arrived, she would generously serve them and even pack up the leftover food to send with them. At that time, new clothes and rubber shoes could only be obtained during the Lunar New Year or Chuseok, so·we eagerly awaited these holidays. My younger sister, Jeong-sook, and I would sit next to our mother while she sewed, begging her to buy us nice clothes and shoes. We wanted to wear them to go out and show off to the other kids in the village who had the better clothes and shoes.

Celebrating traditional holidays in Deoksilgol

Whenever my brothers came home during their school vacations and asked for tuition, my mother would go around the village to borrow money, trying to give them as much as she could. The same happened when I was attending the Korea Military Academy. Although the academy provided a stipend for cadets, it wasn't enough even for transportation costs when we went out. Knowing how financially strained we were, my mother would take out the small change she had saved up whenever I went home for the holidays and hand it to me. The bundle of small coins was tightly wrapped with a black rubber band. How precious that money must have been to her. She didn't spend it on what she wanted or on unnecessary things but carefully saved it over time, and now she was giving it to her child as travel money. That money, which had the marks of time on it, was more precious to me than even hundreds of millions of won.

After sending her children away to the city, my mother did all the farm work alone. Her hands, which worked tirelessly in the fields, became rough and calloused. The scars from when she cut her fingers while chopping feed for the ox with a sickle never disappeared throughout her life. I was always concerned about her health, especially when I saw her pressing her stomach with a pestle in the kitchen, suffering from poor digestion. Despite this, she never once visited a hospital and maintained her health throughout her life. My mother was made of tough, unyielding strength.

I had been separated from my mother since I graduated from elementary school. Because we spent so little time together, my mother always worried about her youngest child. When I was leaving for my second tour in the Vietnam War, I departed from Gimpo Airport, and my mother came to see me off. She had come all the way from Deoksilgol to see her child off to Vietnam.

At that time, Gimpo Airport was the only international airport. Since I had no relatives in Seoul, my mother was concerned about whether she could make her way back home alone. Fortunately, I ran into Kim Young-ri's wife, who was a classmate from my military academy (who later became my fourth cousin-in-law) at the airport. She kindly took my mother to her home, let her stay for the night, and promised to send her by train to Daegu, which put my mind at ease.

Seeing the kind beauty of a college-educated woman, my mother asked her to help me find such a virtuous wife, requesting her to act as a matchmaker. Later, when I was engaged, my mother was astonished to realize that the woman who had been so kind to us at the engagement ceremony was the very same person, my fourth cousin-in-law. She often recalled that story whenever she had the chance. My mother's love and affection were deeper than anyone else's. I never saw her gossip about others. She always thought of the less fortunate, extending kindness and love, and her character was one I have inherited. She was the teacher who taught me love and affection through actions.

My mother's wish was to place a seat of honor at the graves of my maternal grandparents. Noticing this, my eldest brother, Cha

Ki-whan, contacted our fourth cousins and maternal uncles to raise funds and installed the seat of honor. My mother, who had saved up her pocket money, contributed all of it, and my older brother also made a large donation to fulfill her wish. Although she was the youngest daughter, my mother demonstrated her deep filial piety through her actions, showing it to her children.

After my father passed away, my eldest brother took care of my mother. I wandered around the country during my military service, so I never had the chance to live with my parents. It was my wish, along with my wife's, to live with my mother.

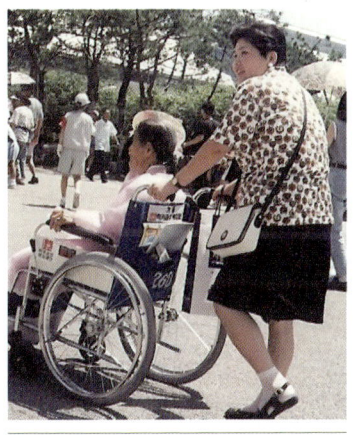 

Jeon Soon-seun and Kim Kyeong-ah   Jeon Soon-seun and Cha Jeong-seok

After becoming a general and settling down in Bucheon, on the outskirts of Seoul, for the sake of our children's studies, we decided to bring my mother to live with us. With my eldest brother's consent, my wife and I took care of my mother in her later years.

At 89 years old, my mother was in good health and had never caught a cold. Even while I was taking care of her, she would do small chores around the house and found joy in them every day. I took her to the senior center and entrusted her to the elderly, bringing rice cakes, fruits, and other offerings. Since my mother was good at socializing, she became popular among the village elders, playing card games like Hwatu and contributing small amounts of money, such as 10-won coins. Sujin and Jeongseok also loved and respected their grandmother, so our family was always filled with happy laughter. My mother loved reading books. It was my wife's task to go to the bookstore and pick out books like *Chunhyangjeon* and *Hong Gildongjeon*, which my mother enjoyed. In the evenings, she liked watching historical dramas. If she couldn't watch them, we would record the episodes and show them to her, which she greatly appreciated.

However, after turning 90, my mother's strength began to fade, and she started feeling discomfort when moving around. I had to carry her on my back when I wanted to take her to the local restaurant to buy her favorite food. My mother liked going out while being carried on my back. As I felt her growing lighter on my back, I couldn't help but feel a deep sense of sorrow and regret.

By the time she turned 93, my mother often said that everyone she knew had passed away and that she was the only one left. She would say that it was time for her to go. She would also mention that she met certain people in her dreams who kept beckoning her, and she felt that she needed to prepare to go. My wife and I, hoping that she could live to 100, did everything we could to care for her with all our love and devotion.

My mother asked to be sent to Daegu to pass away in her hometown. At my eldest brother's house, my sister-in-law had also passed away, and there was no one to take care of her, so it was not possible to send her there. We planned to discuss it a few days later when the whole family gathered for her birthday. However, on December 1, 2000, she passed away. The day before she left, my mother asked my wife to bathe her. We would bathe her once a week, but she requested one even though it was not the usual day. After my wife bathed her, she changed into new clothes and went to sleep. She had a good dinner, watched her favorite soap opera, and then went to sleep.

I usually left for work early in the morning. Since traffic in

Seoul was heavy, leaving early from home helped save time and fuel and reduce stress. After I left for work, just like on regular days, my wife would bring the breakfast tray into my mother's room. But on this day, my mother was still sleeping. When my wife placed the tray next to her and tried to wake her up, she felt cold. In a panic, my wife called 119, and the doctor who arrived confirmed that she had passed away several hours earlier.

The mortuary of Jeon Soon-seun at Samsung Seoul Hospital

I received a call from my wife at the office and rushed home, but calling my mother desperately did no good. I had heard that some people pass away in their sleep, but I experienced firsthand the scene of my mother passing away peacefully while seemingly asleep. My mother, who had never once been to the hospital and had always been healthy, quietly passed away in her sleep. That image of her remained with me for a long time and never left my memory.

After transferring my mother to Samsung Medical Center, I informed relatives in Daegu, Ulsan, and Busan. We held the funeral in Seoul and then brought her to Deoksilgol to be laid to rest beside my father's grave in the family cemetery. To mourn the virtuous mother, people gathered in large numbers. We placed her in a sunny spot at the cemetery and returned home, where I spent the entire day crying, feeling empty and regretful as I looked at the empty room where my mother had once been.

5. Childhood Friends Who Shared Everything Down to the Last Candy

After my mother passed away and I began sorting through her belongings, memories of my hometown came rushing back like scenes from a film. Behind our house stood a large sacred guardian tree. In the summer, it was a playground for mischievous children who climbed its branches to catch cicadas and swing from its limbs. Once a year, the villagers held a ritual at the sacred guardian tree, adorning it with red, blue, and yellow cloth strips. Instead of holding the ritual at a *seonangdang* (village deity shrine), the villagers laid a straw mat beneath the sacred guardian tree and performed the *seonangje* (tutelary deity ritual) on the first day of the lunar new year. The officiant was chosen each year among the village's oldest and most blameless members. The food was prepared at the officiant's house, and the offerings, once ready, were carried to the sacred guardian tree by the village women, where the men would arrange them in front of the tree. The costs were covered by money pooled from the village, and the ritual prayer was composed and read aloud by my father, who was well-versed in classical Chinese literature.

Burning the *Daljip** on Jeongwol Daeboreum

*Daljip is a traditional large wooden structure built during *Jeongwol Daeboreum*, the first full moon of the lunar new year in Korea. It is set on fire in a ritual meant to bring good luck, a bountiful harvest, and drive away evil spirits for the coming year.

On the full moon of the first lunar month, we made a *daljip* (a traditional bonfire structure) and set it ablaze, hoping for a prosperous harvest in the coming year. The *daljip* was constructed by gathering pine branches and forming a large hut-like structure. Once set on fire, the flames would rise toward the sky, accompanied by smoke.

As the fire blazed, the sound of traditional percussion instruments like the drum, *jing*, and *kkwaenggwari* (Korean tranditional gongs) would stir up the festive atmosphere. During this time, I would play with the other village children, attaching a string to a tin can filled with charcoal and spinning it in a circle, engaging in a traditional game of *jibulnori* (a type of fire play) throughout the night. The area in front of the house where the bonfire was set, next to the rice paddy field, became our winter playground. After the harvest, we would slide down the empty fields on sleds made from wire and wooden boards, playing with *gwan-solpaengi* (a spinning top).

Moving pictures and the circus came to our village several imes a year. Since it was the era of silent films, the passionate and captivating voice of the narrator often brought tears to the eyes of the village women. When the circus arrived, my mischievous friends and I would secretly sneak under the circus tent, only to be caught by the director and punished for the entire day.

At this time, Deoksilgol had no electricity. On special days, like during rituals, we would light an kerosene lamp in the main room, and the entire family would work under its bright glow. Because the lamp used oil, the glass would become covered in soot, requiring frequent cleaning. Cleaning the kerosene lamp was my responsibility. Still, I took great pride in knowing that my work brought bright light to the entire family. Here, I learned the timeless wisdom of finding fulfillment in working for others and living a life of purpose. Farming often continued late into the night, and even when we were gathering crops in the yard, we worked under the glow of the kerosene lamp. Even without electricity, the light from the lamp added both brightness and a sense of romance to the countryside.

Across the way in the village of Yangchon, my first cousin once removed was the township head and also ran a distillery. At the time, owning both a distillery and a rice mill marked someone as well-off in the countryside. One day, a group of mischievous boys sneaked into his house and stole some leftover mash from the brewing process. We got drunk and spent the entire day stumbling around in a tipsy stupor. Among those friends, my closest childhood companions were Samdol (Cha Ki-hyo) and Imani (Cha Jong-hyung). Samdol, a second cousin, a year older than I, was warm-hearted and sincere. Imani was fearless and full of adventurous spirit—he could easily climb dangerous rocky paths and always led the way when we went to pick azaleas in the mountains. We all liked him for his dedication and quick wit.

We mischievous boys loved heading to the stream to bathe and wash straw mats, only to be caught by the owner and run away laughing. Sometimes, while catching cicadas in the zelkova tree in front of our house, a sudden downpour would send us scrambling into the nearby taro field, where we'd pluck the broad leaves and use them as makeshift umbrellas as we ran home. In the countryside, there were no soccer balls. For soccer-loving kids like us, the day a pig was slaughtered in the village was also the day of a big soccer match. On ordinary days, we bundled up straw ropes to play in the alley, but when a pig was butchered, we'd inflate its bladder to use as a ball—a major event for the local boys.

With no playground equipment back then, playing marbles and slap-match games with paper cards were among our favorite pastimes. We tore up any scrap paper we could find to make the cards. Since my older brothers were studying in Busan, our house was full of old books. I used pages from those to make the strongest cards and often won the most in games. I was so good at it that I became known as the king of marbles and card games in the village.

Seodang (a traditional village school)

At the village *seodang* (a traditional village school), the *hunjang* (classical Chinese teacher) taught us Chinese characters. Even before entering elementary school, I attended the seodang and studied alongside Samdoli and Imani, who were my classmates there. But we mischievous boys were more interested in playing than studying, even at the seodang, so we often ended up getting our calves caned with a bamboo stick by the hunjang.

Though my childhood friends and I sometimes quarreled when we didn't see eye to eye, we also built our friendship by sharing something as simple as a single piece of candy. After coming home from the seodang, we would take the cattle out to graze. Each of us would lead our family's cow to the fields or hills, and this time became something to look forward to, as it gave us the freedom to gather and play with our friends. We would let the cows graze freely across the mountains and fields, then bring them home again in the evening.

After letting the cattle graze freely, we young herders would spend our time playing marbles and slap-match, or digging up bellflower roots and arrowroot, completely losing track of time. Once, our cow slipped on a large rock and injured its leg. I felt even more pain than if I had been hurt myself, and thanks to my devoted care, the cow made a full recovery in a short time. My affection and devotion for our cow ran deeper than anyone could imagine.

My beloved yellow cow was sold by my father at the five-day market across the river to cover my brother's school tuition. I can't describe how much I cried that day, hiding under my blanket. I locked the door and wept until my eyes were swollen. Once a bond is formed, even an animal can be loved as deeply as a person. I refused to eat and cried for several days, and eventually, my father brought home a calf to comfort me. Growing up in such circumstances, I engraved in my heart the lifelong philosophy of "loving others and never deceiving oneself" in pursuit of eternal life.

6. Outbreak of the Korean War and My Childhood

The Korean War broke out on June 25, 1950, when I was six years old, spending my early childhood in Deoksilgol. The war began at 4 a.m. on a Sunday, as North Korean forces illegally crossed the 38th parallel, led by T-34 tanks. Since it was the weekend, many South Korean soldiers were on leave, and the Army Headquarters in Yongsan held a dance party attended by generals and their spouses. The South Korean military, caught off guard, urgently recalled soldiers on leave through radio broadcasts that Sunday morning. I remember waking up, turning on the radio, and hearing the announcer's panicked voice ringing in my ears.

"North Korean forces have illegally invaded across the 38^{th}parallel!"

"All South Korean troops, return to your units immediately! Return to your units!"

The radio broadcast declared a state of emergency across the entire soldiers from neighboring houses who had been on leave hurriedly returned to their units. I was only six years old, too young to understand what war even meant, but I had a sinking feeling that something ominous was unfolding. The radio kept streaming news reports:

"Our brave troops are crushing enemy tanks with their own bodies in the Munsan area and advancing north!"

"In Ongjin, the 17th Regiment is pushing forward toward Haeju!"

"Our forces will continue advancing—lunch in Pyongyang, and dinner in Sinuiju!"

Despite the North Korean army's overwhelming advance, the radio broadcasts continued to repeat false reports to reassure the public. In the end, these misleading announcements prevented many Seoul citizens from fleeing south and left them to suffer under communist rule. The North Korean forces occupied Mia-ri in Seoul just three days after the war began. At the time, the South Korean army did not have a single tank. No matter how many times soldiers fired their M1 rifles, the enemy tanks kept rolling forward like monsters—there was simply no way to stop them. Some soldiers even climbed onto enemy tanks with grenades in hand, opened the hatches, and threw the grenades inside—sacrificing themselves in desperate acts of resistance.

Outbreak of the Korean War on June 25, 1950

In the face of relentless advance by North Korean tanks, General Chae Byeong-deok, the Chief of Staff of the South Korean Army, ordered Colonel Choi Chang-sik, the chief engineer, to blow up the Han River bridges. Then, the army headquarters moved to Siheung in Gyeonggi Province. With the destruction of the bridges, South Korean forces could not cross the Han River and were annihilated north of it. At that time,

Seoul had a population of 1.5 million. Of them, 1 million fled the city, while 500,000 were unable to cross the Han River and stayed behind, suffering under the communist occupation until Seoul was recaptured.

After the Han River bridge was blown up, General Douglas MacArthur, who was in Tokyo, flew in a plane to Suwon Airfield and inspected the southern bank of the Han River. Realizing that the South Korean military alone could not stop the North Korean advance, he called U.S. President Harry S. Truman and suggested immediately deploying U.S. forces stationed in Japan to the Korea. After receiving the report from General MacArthur, President Truman, who was vacationing at his home in Missouri, immediately returned to Washington. Following a meeting of the National Security Council, he decided to send the 24th U.S. Infantry Division, stationed in Japan, to the Korea and to deploy additional U.S. military forces to Korea to prevent the communist takeover of South Korea, which the United Nations had recognized as the sole legitimate government of the Korean Peninsula. Meanwhile, the radio continued to broadcast news about the war.

"U.S. troops will come to help us. Citizens, please rest assured."

"General MacArthur has inspected the Han River, and UN forces will soon enter our country."

The Ruins of Seoul

The United States requested support from the United Nations for the Korean War, and on June 28, 1950, the UN Security Council held a meeting to decide to deploy UN forces to stop the communist invasion. Sixteen countries participated in the Korean War under the UN banner, including the United States, the United Kingdom, France, Canada, Australia, New Zealand, the Netherlands, the Philippines, Turkey, Thailand, Greece,

South Africa, Belgium, Luxembourg, Colombia, and Ethiopia.[1]

The UN requested that the United States appoint a UN Commander, and in response, the United States appointed General Douglas MacArthur as the commander of UN forces. Upon his appointment, General MacArthur immediately appointed General Walton H. Walker as the commander of the 8th U.S. Army, entrusting him with the command of ground forces in the Korean War. Later, General Walker was killed in action during the Battle of Uijeongbu. The Walker Hill Hotel in Seoul was named in honor of General Walker."

At this time, President Syngman Rhee, following the principle of unified command, handed over the operational control of the South Korean military to General Douglas MacArthur, the UN Commander, who was already in charge of the forces from 16 UN member countries. With the operational control of the South Korean military and the command of all UN forces, General MacArthur sent the advance unit of the 24th U.S. Infantry Division, the Smith Task Force, to Osan in July 1950. However, they were unable to withstand the powerful tanks of the

---

[1] Cha Kimoon, The Just War Through Modern History (Seoul: Yeoknak Publishing, 2008), pp. 337-338.

advancing North Korean army. Soon after, the main force of the 24th U.S. Infantry Division arrived, but they were overwhelmed at the defense line along the Geumgang River in Daejeon, and General William F. Dean, the commander of the 24th Division, was taken prisoner.

The North Korean army, which continued pushing southward, reached the Nakdong River line in early August 1950. Even in my hometown, Deoksilgol, located along the Nakdong River, the North Korean soldiers arrived. My older brothers, who were high school students, were home for summer vacation. After a long time, they took me to the fields to wash and catch catfish and loaches. Then, soldiers who appeared to be from the advance unit of the North Korean army approached us. They were wearing muddy uniforms and camouflaged with leaves from trees. One of the soldiers, carrying a submachine gun and a rifle on his shoulder, asked in a Pyongyang dialect:

"Where is the Nakdong River?"

"Just go that way."

"When did the police leave, and where did they go?"

"I don't know."

"Do you know where the South Korean troops are?"

"I don't know."

"You little brats, you don't know anything!"

Before long, countless North Korean soldiers lined up along the northern and western ridges of the mountains and moved toward the Nakdong River. The North Korean troops that entered Deoksilgol at this time were from the 4th Division of the 1st Corps. The 4th Division, led by Major General Lee Gwon-mu, was called the 'Seoul Division' because it was the first to capture Seoul. The 4th Division also included Korean-Chinese soldiers who had fought alongside Mao Zedong's forces during China's unification.

Meanwhile, in opposition to the North Korean 4th Division, the U.S. 24th Division, commanded by Major General John H. Church, was deployed across the Nakdong River in the areas of Hyeonpung and Changnyeong. General Church, who had served as the forward liaison officer, became the commander of the U.S. 24th Division after Major General Dean, who had been captured by the North Korean forces in Daejeon. This division, stationed from Hyeonpung to Namji, the junction of the Nam River, still felt the aftermath of its defeat in Daejeon. The divisions were only about 40% reinforced to their original strength, and each regiment could only maintain two battalions.

Defending the Nakdong River

General Church, judging that North Korean forces would approach Changnyeong by mid-August, used the experience gained from the Battle of Daejeon to evacuate civilians east of the Changnyeong-Yangsan line. At the same time, he ordered the tens of thousands of refugees attempting to cross the Nakdong River to halt their crossing. With superior air power over the enemy, the UN forces bombed large buildings, such as schools, where the enemy was likely gathering. UN fighter planes also bombed Deoksilgol daily.

When the bombing became intense, our family would take shelter under the rock beneath the tree near the village shrine, following my father. One time, my second-oldest brother, Cha Ki-hong, had been taking a nap and couldn't catch up with us. When he finally made his way towards the tree, a fighter plane spotted him and opened fire with its machine guns. My father instinctively pushed us into the trunk of the tree and held us tightly, protecting us with his body. It was my father's natural instinct to fight to protect his family, and because of that, we all managed to escape unharmed once the bombing ceased. The school that had been bombed was engulfed in flames, and the bodies of dozens of villagers lay scattered. As a child, I found it fascinating to watch the fighter planes swoop low above us and drop bombs. Afterward, I cried and begged to go with the other children to collect the spent shell casings. The .50 caliber shell casings were used for various purposes. We would melt them down to make farming tools or exchange them for taffy when a taffy seller came to town. Back in the days when we had no toys, collecting shell casings was one of our greatest pleasures.

Amidst the constant bombardment by the UN forces' fighter planes, the North Korean troops that entered Deoksilgol forcibly took all the young men from the village, calling them part of the "volunteer army." The village leaders were also taken and labeled as tainted by capitalist ideology. My older brother, who had come of age, and my father, who was considered a local leader, became targets of the North Korean troops and had no choice but to flee to a distant refuge.

UN military aircraft

However, the escape route to the south was blocked, so we had no choice but to hide in the mountains behind the village. My father and older brother climbed up to Danaman Mountain behind the village, where they dug a tunnel to take refuge. Holding onto the hem of my mother's skirt as she carried rice and side dishes to bring to the family hiding in the mountains, I followed her, feeling like we were going on a picnic. From the mountain, the distant sounds of gunfire and the thick smoke rising from the Haphyeon area felt like scenes from a movie.

"Vroom! Vroom!"

"Shhh~ ~"

"Bang! Bang!"

The sound of machine guns blazing from the fighter jets pierced through the air, deafening the ears. Watching the fighter jets fly low over the foot of the mountain, even as a young child, I had a sudden impulse to become a soldier and fight on the battlefield like that. The North Korean troops, lacking proper communication methods, sent signals to each other by lighting beacons on various mountains. As a result, pillars of fire rose high into the night sky from the high mountains, and during the day, smoke billowed up from one mountain to another.

After delivering food to my father and brothers, who were hiding in the mountains, I came back down with my mother and found that a North Korean company had occupied our house. They had slaughtered all the pigs and chickens in the house and demanded that rice be cooked for them. Since my family was hiding in the mountains, my mother had no choice but to comply with whatever the North Korean soldiers ordered. During the Nakdong River battle, our house became their company headquarters.

After eating all the livestock and rice from our house, they went around the village, catching cows and pigs, and asked my mother to cook rice for them. While the rice was being cooked, I became fascinated as I touched the submachine guns and rifles of the North Korean soldiers who were resting on the main floor of the house. They bragged that they had come down from the 38th parallel to the Nakdong River without firing a single shot. This was because the South Korean army was completely unprepared for war, and as a result, they were unable to stop the North Korean forces and were pushed all the way down to the Nakdong River. The North Korean army, which had to cross the Nakdong River, which had a width of 200 to 500 meters, lacked proper crossing equipment and had to use rafts. They gathered all the trees and planks from the village to make the rafts. They even took the wooden door from our house, so Deoksilgol became a village where every home had no doors.

In our village, my cousin, Cha Ki-bun, who was known as the most beautiful woman, was a teacher at Deokgok Elementary School. The North Korean soldiers took my cousin to the battalion headquarters in the lower village and forced her to serve them. At that time, my father and eldest brother, Cha Ki-whan, were captured from the mountain and taken to the battalion headquarters. The charge against them was that they had spread the news that the UN forces would soon arrive and were considered reactionary elements due to their relatively good living as local elites.

My father and eldest brother were subjected to all kinds of torture by the North Korean soldiers. They gave a shovel to my brother and ordered him to dig a grave, intending to bury my father alive. When he refused to obey this order, they threatened to execute my brother. There was a dispute among the soldiers, as some of them argued that killing innocent people was unjust. A conflict arose between the party officials and the tactical officers.

Incheon Landing Operation

Amidst this chaos, my cousin, who had been dragged to the anti-communist facility and was about to be raped, was saved by my brother, who risked his life to rescue her, causing an uproar throughout the entire barracks. This incident was reported to the North Korean military command, and following the orders of their superiors, my father, brother, and cousin were released. However, the immense suffering my cousin endured caused her to lose her sanity, and tragically, she eventually passed away.

General MacArthur conducted the Incheon Landing Operation on September 15, 1950, to lead the stalemated front at the Nakdong River to victory. When this operation was initially planned, many people opposed it. This was because Incheon had an extensive tidal range, shallow waters, and was a mudflat, making it difficult to dock landing craft, thus not ideal for a landing operation. In response, General MacArthur argued, "The very reason that many oppose it is the reason I am landing at Incheon. Because of these challenges, the enemy will likely have weak coastal defenses, allowing for a surprise landing." Ultimately, as General MacArthur predicted, the Incheon Landing Operation was carried out and achieved great success.

With the success of the Incheon Landing Operation, the North Korean forces were severed at the waist and their supply lines were cut off, forcing them to retreat north from the Nakdong River line. The UN forces, in cooperation with the units that had landed at Incheon, completely encircled and destroyed the enemy. As a result, most of the North Korean troops were annihilated, and those who could not escape north retreated into Jirisan Mountain, where they became guerrillas and engaged in partisan activities behind the lines until the ceasefire.

On September 15, 1950, the UN forces successfully executed the Incheon Landing Operation, and on September 28, they recaptured Seoul. After liberating Seoul, the UN forces reached the 38th parallel, and there was a division of opinion between the South Korean and UN forces on whether to continue advancing north. South Korea wanted to continue pushing forward and unify the country, while the United States and the UN hesitated to attack north of the 38th parallel due to concerns over China's potential involvement.

Amid these conflicting opinions, President Syngman Rhee issued an order for the South Korean military to attack the north, even independently. Following his command, the South Korean 3rd Division, stationed in the Sokcho area, broke through the 38th parallel and launched an attack northward on October 1, 1950. As the attack advanced northward, the North Korean forces, having already suffered significant losses at the Nakdong

River line due to the Incheon Landing Operation, were swiftly overwhelmed by the South Korean assault. As the South Korean forces advanced north, the United States and the UN forces had no choice but to follow. To commemorate the breach of the 38th parallel, South Korea declared October 1st as Armed Forces Day.

The allied forces that had broken through the 38th parallel advanced northward with unstoppable momentum, occupying Pyongyang on October 20 and reaching the Yalu River on October 25. The UN forces deployed a large-scale parachute unit in the Sukcheon area north of Pyongyang in an attempt to encircle the city and capture Kim Il-sung, but he had already fled to the Kangye region, leaving Pyongyang virtually empty.

ROK forces breaking through the 38th Parallel

The allied forces that had reached the Amnok River encountered an unexpected Chinese army along the riverbank on October 26, 1950. In order to evade UN aerial reconnaissance, 300,000 Chinese troops entered North Korea by marching only at night. Unaware of China's intervention, the UN forces were unable to withstand the overwhelming human wave tactics of the suddenly appearing Chinese army. No matter how many bullets were fired, the waves of Chinese soldiers—armed only with spiked grenades—kept advancing over the bodies of their fallen comrades. In the end, the UN forces were pushed back by the human wave attacks and had to retreat south, allowing Seoul to fall back into communist hands. This retreat is known as the January 4th Retreat.

Hungnam Evacuation Operation

When the UN forces were retreating, the U.S. Marine Corps 1st Division, which had advanced to the Geumagowon, withdrew toward Changjin Lake and then retreated to Busan by ship from Hungnam. On Christmas Eve, December 24, 1950, as the U.S. Marine Corps 1st Division came out to Hungnam to board naval ships, refugees gathered in a chaotic scene, trying to board the ships as well.[2]

In the end, 100,000 refugees were boarded onto the ships and evacuated together. The song "Be Strong, Geumsun," which depicts this scene, became a hit for a long time and was sung by many people.

> In the cold winds of Hungnam pier,
>
> where snowstorms swirl,
>
> I called out with all my might, looking for you,
>
> Geumsun, where have you gone, lost and wandering
>
> I came alone after the Chinese intervention,
>
> shedding tears of blood.
>
> What am I to do now with no family or relatives

---

2   Opt. cit., pp.343~345.

> I am now a peddler in the Kukje Market.
>
> Geumsun, I miss you so much,
>
> I long for my hometown dreams.
>
> On the railing of Yeongdo Bridge,
>
> only a crescent moon rises, lonely and still.

At that time, most of the public buildings, including schools, were destroyed by bombing and burned down, so we hung a blackboard on a tree and spread a mat on the ground to study. After class, we picked up shell casings and nails from the ashes of the school floor. This was because each school had received orders to collect scrap metal and donate it to the government.

Relief supplies such as clothes and milk arrived from the United States and were distributed to the students. The clothes that Americans wore were so large that the shirts fit like oversized jackets, and the shoes were as big as boats, so some of the children dragged them along as they walked. The powdered milk came in large drums, and some children choked while drinking water after putting the powder in their mouths and had to be taken to the hospital.

At that time, the men, after only practicing pulling the trigger when they enlisted, were sent straight into combat.

The new recruits, just enlisted, had lives as fleeting as that of mayflies. The men from our village wore shoulder straps to mark their enlistment and left their homes, receiving a farmer's music farewell from the villagers who came as far as the village outskirts. Looking over the fence, the women from the neighboring houses shed endless tears as they watched their husbands and sons take their final journey. The song "The Wife's Destiny" by Baek Seol-hee, which depicted this scene, also became popular.

In March 1951, the allied forces regained the 38th parallel, and the tedious trench warfare continued. As the front lines stalled at the 38th parallel, General MacArthur suggested dropping atomic bombs on Manchuria and pursuing northern unification. Following the U.S. policy of rejecting any escalation of the war, General MacArthur was relieved of his duties as the UN Commander on April 11, 1951. Before retiring, he said these famous words in the U.S. Congress: "Old soldiers never die; they just fade away." General Matthew Bunker Ridgway was appointed as the new UN Commander. As the U.S. presidential election was approaching, the United States was eager to end the Korean War quickly.

The armistice agreement signed at Panmunjom

During this period, Soviet representative Yakov Aleksandrovich Malik proposed an armistice in a speech at the United Nations, and the armistice talks began in Kaesong on July 10, 1951. The communist forces insisted on holding the armistice talks in Kaesong, which was under the control of the North Korean army at the time, and thus the first armistice talks were held there. The reason the communist forces insisted on Kaesong was that it was located south of the 38th parallel, under the control of the North Korean army. Since the UN forces were stronger than the communist forces, they wanted to hold the talks in Kaesong to prevent losing control of the area.

While the talks continued, they were delayed due to the

issue of prisoner exchanges. However, on March 5, 1953, with the death of Soviet leader Joseph Vissarionovich Stalin, who had been pursuing a hardline policy regarding the Korean War, the armistice talks made rapid progress. The two sides first exchanged wounded prisoners, and then on July 27, 1953, at 10:00 AM, the ceasefire agreement was signed at Panmunjom.

The three years of the fratricidal Korean War left the entire Korean Peninsula, both North and South, in ruins and caused immense human casualties. The loss of combat forces alone was staggering, with the UN forces, including the South Korean military, losing 180,000 lives, while the communist forces suffered 520,000 casualties from the North Korean army and 900,000 from the Chinese army. Additionally, during the war, 990,000 civilians in South Korea lost their lives or were injured.[3]

Such a tragedy of fratricidal conflict must never occur again on this land. We must recall the proverb "If you want peace, prepare for war," and concentrate all efforts on national security to prevent war.

---

3   Opt. cit., pp. 350~351.

7. Six Years of Excellence and Perfect Attendance at Deokgok Elementary School

During the intense period of the war, with the frontlines pushing back and forth from the Nakdong River to the Amnokgang River, I entered Deokgok Elementary School. Deokgok Elementary School, which boasts a rich history and tradition, was established on September 25, 1926, as Deokgok Public Primary School and has produced many talented individuals. Upon entering elementary school, I began to move ahead of other students, building on the knowledge of Korean and arithmetic I had learned from my older brothers. As soon as I started, I read through the textbooks without hesitation, and soon rumors spread among the students and teachers about my academic abilities.

Once, my 4th grade teacher, Mr. Cha Gi-bun, called me and asked me to read from the 4th grade Korean textbook in front of all the students in her classroom. Of course, she had me, a first-year student, read in front of the class to motivate her students, but I also felt somewhat embarrassed to read in front of the older students.

As a first-year student, I read through the 4th grade Korean textbook without hesitation, which surprised the older students and made me popular among the girls. In the countryside, education for women was conservative. During the Korean War, it was even harder for girls to enter school on time. In our class, some girls had missed the proper age for schooling and enrolled late, so their ages were 2 to 3 years older than the boys. Kim Myeong-seon, Na Gap-chul, Na Myeong-ja, Na Sook-i, Park Jeong-ae, and Seo Gi-bun were all taller and had a more mature appearance, looking so grown-up that they seemed ready to be married off. Only Na Gap-yeon and Park Ok-seon were around our age, and the rest treated the boys like younger siblings, making them feel more like distant classmates from another world.

Since the boys were physically and age-wise different from the girls, we often played only with those who were around our age and could communicate easily. Particularly, my close friends—Kang Shin-chan, Kim Bok-gi, Kim Jeong-yeol, Koo Gi-young, Koo Ja-seon, Noh Yeong-hoon, Seo Jae-cheon, Seo Jae-hong, Seong Dong-han, Lee Han-chul, Im Ssang-hyo, Jeong Su-jin, Jeong Eun-mok, Cha Yeong-seob, Cha Jong-hyeong, Choi Dong-gil, and Choi Jang-seok—spent a lot of time together after school, visiting each other's homes, eating together, and even sleeping over, building a strong friendship during our time at Deokgok Elementary School.

During my time at Deokgok Elementary School
(I am the fourth person from the left in the second row)

When friends came to our friends' houses, parents treated their kids' friends with even more kindness than their own, so sometimes I felt like my friends' parents were like mine. We often lost track of time when we played together and sometimes stayed up all night. There were many occasions when we were late and had to receive group punishment.

I would bring my lunchbox to school, but by the time lunch hour came, it was already empty. After the first period, one-third was gone; after the second period, another third was gone;

and after the third period, yet another third was gone. By the time lunch arrived, the lunchbox was completely empty. The teacher would have anyone who ate their lunch raise their hand and stand in punishment until lunchtime ended. Still, the joy of eating lunch was greater than the joy of studying. During winter, there was no oil for the heater, so we would go to the mountains to collect rotting tree stumps and pine needles to make a fire. While the boys went to the mountains to gather wood, the girls cleaned and waited for the boys to return with the firewood. However, the boys often got distracted while collecting wood and got lost in the deep forest chasing rabbits, unaware of the setting sun. At times like these, the principal would wait at the foot of the mountain, and with a furious look, he would give us a group punishment.

During the war, the classroom was destroyed by bombing, so we studied under the plane trees on the school grounds. We hung a blackboard on a tree branch and laid a mat on the dirt ground. We studied while listening to the sounds of cicadas.

"Chirp, chirp,chirp…"

In time with the cicada's cries, we memorized the multiplication tables under the shade of the trees. When it rained, we would go into the storage shed to study. Despite the circumstances, my desire to study was stronger than anyone else's. The level of my studies was no less than that of the students in the city.

Childhood Friends at Deokgok Elementary School
(I am the one wearing the hat, fifth from the left in the second row).

A student named Jeong Hwa-ja transferred from Busan to Deokgok Elementary School. Having grown up in a large city, she was sophisticated and dressed well. Her father had run for the National Assembly three times, and their family was well-off with a respectable background. Jeong Hwaja, with her fair skin and elegant demeanor, was undoubtedly the most popular among us. The boys competed to impress her, trying to stand out. We, the rural kids with faces darkened by the sun, couldn't help but notice our differences. However, there was not much difference between us when it came to studying. Although she had studied well in Busan, her academic level was similar to ours, which gave us a sense of pride and made her a worthy, friendly competitor.

In the fall, the school's autumn sports festival was held in the schoolyard, which was covered in blooming cosmos flowers. Pine branches from the mountain were used to create an arch at the school gate, and national flags fluttered in the sports field. Folk music groups from each village gathered to showcase their talents. On this day, thousands of people, including students, parents, and village residents, came together to create an atmosphere like a festival.

Fall Sports Day at the Elementary School

We eagerly looked forward to the fall sports day for several days. We practiced various talent shows over many days to show our parents everything we had learned at school. On the day of the event, we were divided into the blue and white teams, and along with our parents, we competed in events like three-legged races, rolling large balls, 100-meter sprints, and relays, proudly showcasing our skills. My mother packed special kimbap on Sports Day with boiled sweet potatoes and chestnuts. The taste of eating our lunch with some soup under the shade of a tree was so delicious that we wouldn't have noticed if anything had happened.

When we were in the 6th grade, we went on a school trip to Tongyeong. The idea of going on a school trip from Deokgok to Hansando in Tongyeong was something most people wouldn't have even considered. However, we had made plans for a long time, got permission from our parents, and set off on a long-distance school trip. Back then, buses were scarce, so we rented a truck and traveled on an unpaved road for 10 hours. The boys and girls, covered in dust, were jostled around every time the truck bumped, making the journey even more fun.

Graduating from Deokgok Elementary School, I had perfect attendance for all 6 years and graduated as the top student in the school. I received the highest honor, the Gyeongsangnam-do Superintendent's Award. I was also the class president every year. In 3rd grade, I was once overtaken by my rival, Han Nam-sik, but I continued. In 6th grade, I demonstrated leadership as the school president. Despite the rivalry, Han Nam-sik and I remained close friends, often consulting each other during difficult times. He stayed my close friend until he passed from liver cancer at the Ilsan Cancer Center.

Graduated as the top student of Deokgok Elementary School

After graduating from Deokgok Elementary School, I entered middle school in Daegu. Going to study in Daegu from Deoksilgol was a significant event. Most students could not attend middle school, and those slightly better off financially usually attended nearby Okya Middle School or Hapcheon Middle School.

In this environment, it was through the enthusiasm of my parents, who wanted to provide me with an education, as well as my desire for learning, that I was able to go to Daegu to study. At that time, I had no connections in Daegu, and it was my first time leaving for a distant place to study.

Chapter 2

•

| My Youth Away from Home |

1. From Deoksilgol to Daegu

In an era when transportation was underdeveloped, the means of getting from Deoksilgol to Daegu were inadequate. It took over two hours to reach Ibang, where buses operated between Jinju and Daegu, running twice or thrice a day. At that time, buses operated by companies like Cheonil and Gyeongjeon Bus were in service, but the bus schedules were irregular, and we had to wait for hours by the roadside, covered in dust. Each bus had an assistant who supported the driver. The assistant's role was to start the engine using a hand crank if it stalled during the trip, collect fares from passengers, and provide guidance. During flooding of the Nakdong River, cars couldn't pass, and we had to walk all the way to Hyeonpung, a journey that took more than four hours.

Studying in the city from the countryside was not an easy

task, especially with the tuition fees. My family was considered wealthy in the village, owning significant land and employing several servants for farming. However, to cover my older brothers' school expenses, we sold our fields, cattle, and pigs, and the only thing left was a small piece of land that was barely enough to sustain us. Despite the lack of resources to send me to school, my parents couldn't break my determination after I graduated from elementary school at the top of my class. I promised them I would earn a scholarship to cover my tuition if they could send me food. At 14, I left for Daegu without any concrete plans.

My father, who had an exceptional passion for educating his children, thought highly of me and decided to carry the rice for my meals as we went to Daegu together. It was my first time going to Daegu, but by chance, I ran into a distant relative. This relative, acquainted with my father, took us to his home, explained the situation in Daegu, and offered us a vacant room at a modest monthly rent. This house was conveniently located right next to the school I would attend, making it an ideal location for my studies. I also felt a sense of comfort knowing that I was with family in the unfamiliar city of Daegu. Since our situation didn't allow for boarding, I decided to live on my own and unpacked my belongings in that house. While living alone, we used briquettes for heating, and grilling mackerel over the briquette fire became one of the best dishes I could enjoy. Mackerel was the cheapest among meats, but nothing tasted better than mackerel grilled over briquettes. My school fees and allowance were covered by the scholarships I received from the school, and the rent was paid in rice sent by my father.

Once, after summer vacation ended and the new school term began, my father and I were on our way to Daegu carrying a sack of rice when we encountered a flood. The Nakdong River had overflowed, blocking the roads and preventing buses from running. We took a boat across Ibang and then traveled to Guji to see if Daegu-bound buses would arrive, but it was a wasted effort. We had no choice but to walk to Hyeonpung, several kilometers away, with our heavy load. Only when we reached Hyeonpung did we finally find a bus to Daegu. However, the rural bus, which came very infrequently, was packed beyond capacity. After explaining our situation, the bus driver reluctantly agreed to let us load the rice onto the bus. My father's dedication deeply motivated me to provide for my education, and I decided to study even harder.

Mackerel grilled over briquettes

When I was in the third year of middle school, my second sister, Cha Jeong-geom, moved to Daegu. She came with her husband, Kim Kong-hee, who had been transferred to Daegu as an elementary school teacher. Since I had been living alone, I decided to stay at my sister's house after her husband came to Daegu. I no longer had to worry about cooking meals, and it was helpful to study with my cousin, Kim Mu-hee, who was two years older than I. Kim Mu-hee was a devout Christian and attended church diligently. At church, he was also learning English from an American missionary. I didn't even know what faith was at the time, but I followed Kim Mu-hee to church and learned English from the missionary. This later became the foundation for my ability to speak English well.

Field trip in the fall of the third year in middle school
(I am the third from the left in the second row)

The electricity situation was poor. Due to power rationing, the electricity would automatically cut off at midnight. Driven by the determination to study hard, I would study by candlelight even after the power went out. I sometimes dozed off and burned my hair with the candle or even my books. To keep myself awake, I would wash my face with cold water and prick my thighs with a needle while studying. As a result, I was able to continue receiving scholarships, which covered my tuition, both in middle school and high school.

As Deoksilgol became part of the Daegu metropolitan area, more and more people from the countryside began moving to Daegu. The urban concentration brought on by industrialization was becoming more palpable. My second eldest brother, Cha Ki-hong, also moved to Daegu. The atmosphere felt less lonely as I began to live with my sister and brother.

After staying at my sister's house, I moved to my brother's house to attend school. During the school breaks, I would return to my hometown with my nieces and nephews. Whenever I returned home after studying in the city, I had to pay respects to the elders in the village. Especially in my hometown, where everyone was practically family, failing to greet the elders would lead to being scolded for poor manners. Apples were famous in Daegu, so I would bring a bundle of apples whenever I returned to my hometown. Since I couldn't greet the elders empty-handed, I would carry apples and a pack of cigarettes, greeting the elders one by one. The village elders were always very pleased. This habit became a form of practical moral education for me.

Once, I rode a bicycle from Daegu to Deoksilgol with my five-year-old nephew, Cha Seok-jin. Moreover, the bicycle was a large cargo bike that my brother used for business purposes. I used the bicycle to save on bus fare, but even now, I think it was reckless. I rode the cargo bike with the child on unpaved roads for a long distance, and when we arrived at my hometown, my parents were quite surprised. Still, spending time with my parents during the holidays in my hometown was the most enjoyable part. When the break ended and I had to leave for Daegu again, I cried endlessly because I didn't want to part with my parents.

My eldest brother, Cha Ki-whan, also moved to Daegu. Now, Daegu has become the place where our family lives together. Everyone, except for my parents, had come to Daegu. My eldest brother bought me a bowl of jajangmyeon. Although I was the first to move to Daegu, I couldn't afford a bowl of jajangmyeon because I was saving money, so I can never forget the taste of the jajangmyeon my brother bought for me then.

2. The Rising Star by Suseong Stream

As a rural kid from Deoksilgol, I had a lot of difficulty deciding which school to attend in Daegu. Initially, I applied to Kyungbuk Middle School, the most prestigious school in Daegu at the time. Since Kyungbuk Middle School was a public school, they did not have an entrance exam, and students were selected based on their elementary school grades. Despite my excellent performance at Deoksilgol Elementary School, where I graduated with honors and perfect attendance over six years, I received a rejection letter due to the disadvantage of coming from a rural school. If I had taken the official entrance exam, I was confident I could have passed, but Kyungbuk Middle School, having never admitted a student from a rural school, failed to recognize the talent from Deoksilgol Elementary School.

After being rejected by Kyungbuk Middle School, I applied to Daeryun Middle School for the second round. Daeryun Middle School was a private school and required an entrance exam. Naturally, I passed the exam with good grades. I achieved the highest score in the history of the school's establishment and proudly became the top student. Daeryun Middle School was located on the flatlands by the Suseong Stream in Daegu. The cold winds from the stream were sharp, as if they were cutting through the skin. Since Daegu is a basin, it is the coldest in winter and the hottest in summer in the entire country. I had a coal stove in my boarding room next to the school, but during the harsh cold, the water in my room froze solid. In these conditions, I studied diligently under the covers, rubbing my hands and feet to keep warm. I knew I had to work even harder than others to maintain the honor of being the top student.

Daeryun School was established on September 15, 1921, by patriotic figures Hong Ju-il, Kim Yeong-seo, and Jeong Un-gi, who were determined to cultivate talented individuals for the independence of the nation. During the Japanese occupation, Japan's educational policy aimed at conforming to their colonial agenda, making it impossible to expect true Korean education. However, the three founders risked their lives to establish a private educational institution for the true education of Koreans. Initially, the school was named Gyeongnam Academy, with Jeong Un-gi as the principal. On October 30, 1940, when Seo Byeong-jo took office as the foundation chairman, the school changed its name to Daeryun School and developed into a prestigious institution dedicated to cultivating individuals committed to the nation's independence.

Daeryun School at the heart of nationalism

When the Korean War broke out, Daeryun School even handed the school in Suseong-dong over to the military and moved to a temporary building in Daebong-dong. However, after the armistice, on October 4, 1954, part of the land and buildings, which had been rented to the U.S. military, were returned.[1] When I attended middle school, some of the school buildings were still being used under the supervision of the military, with barbed wire separating the campus, and the playground was only accessible in a limited manner. Daeryun School was the most rewarding chapter of my life and the guiding light that shaped my worldview. I resolved to become a model student, burning with a passion for learning, aspiring to be a guiding star for my nation and people. I graduated from middle school as the top student in my class. I received many awards, including a clock and a dictionary, along with a certificate of commendation from the Governor of Gyeongsangbuk-do. At the graduation ceremony, my parents from my hometown, my second older brother Cha Ki-hong, my second older sister Cha Jeong-geom, and my brother-in-law Park Dong-gyu attended to congratulate

---

1 Daeryun Alumni Association, Daeryun 80-Year History (Gyeongbuk Printing House, 2001), pp. 102–110.

me, and we took a commemorative photo.

Daeryun Middle School, graduated as the top student
(I am holding a watch prize.)

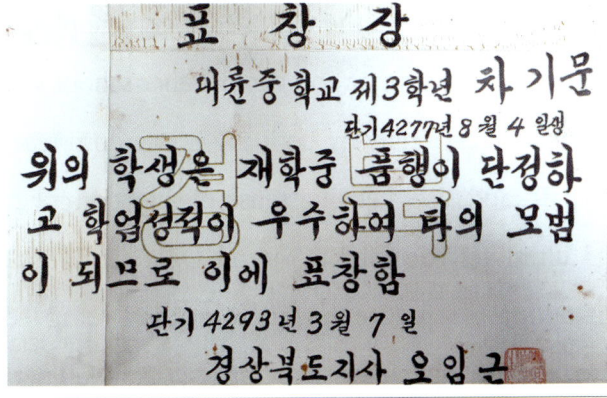

Gyeongbuk Governor's Citation Certificate

After graduating from middle school, I intended to apply to Kyungbuk High School, which was known as the best school in the country at the time. In particular, I was determined to attend Kyungbuk High to make up for not being able to enter Kyungbuk Middle School due to the grading system in the previous school. When I consulted with my teacher about the application, my teacher took me to the principal's office. The principal, almost forcefully, pressured me to attend Daeryun High School, assuring me that if I continued there, I would be guaranteed a scholarship for three years.

The principal believed that sending outstanding students to Daeryun High School would serve as a foundation for the school's growth, and was determined to ensure that I, as the top graduate, continued on to the affiliated high school. Given the atmosphere, it was clear that going to another school was not an option. Persuaded strongly by both my homeroom teacher and the principal—and also feeling a sense of affection for my alma mater—I ultimately decided to attend Daeryun High School. Without taking a separate entrance exam, I returned to my hometown to help my parents with farm work, and later entered the new semester as a scholarship student.

Professor Lee Hyo-sang, who was the dean of the Department of Physics at Kyungpook National University, was appointed acting principal. Meeting Lee Hyo-sang—whose character and capabilities were second to none—allowed me to redefine my outlook on life. In particular, he gave us many memorable lectures. Themes such as "Do not deceive yourself" and "Love others" left a lasting impression.

Daeryun High School Student Council Member
(I am standing second from the left in the back row.)

These two phrases were later established as the school motto of Daeryun and have since taken root as the spirit of all Daeryun alumni. The phrase "Do not deceive yourself" contains a guiding principle for life. If one lives a life without shame, looking up to the heavens without deceiving oneself, that person can be said to have succeeded. All evil in this world begins with self-deception. "Love others" means having a heart that considers and cares for others. A society in which people know how to be considerate of one another can become a utopian paradise on earth. Not deceiving oneself and loving others is the path to caring for oneself, as well as for our society, our nation, and humanity as a whole.

Hansol Lee Hyo-sang graduated from the Department of German Literature at Tokyo Imperial University in 1930. He made his literary debut in 1936 by publishing the poem "Miracle" in Catholic Youth and went on to publish many works, especially research papers related to literature. He entered politics when he was elected to the House of Councillors in 1960 and later served as a member of the 6th and 7th National Assembly and as Speaker of the National Assembly. Lee Hyo-sang was a kind teacher who invited us student council members to his orchard at the foot of Apsan Mountain, where he gave us guidance on school management and lectured us on views of life and the nation.

It was during this time that the Daeryun emblem was also created. In art class, Mr. Park Myeong-jo assigned us to design a new emblem for Daeryun. As we worked on the assignment, we discussed and collaborated with the teacher, and the result of that process became the current Daeryun logo. Because both the school motto and the logo were created during our time at the school, we take greater pride and confidence in being Daeryun alumni than anyone else. The school song, which we sang together in times of both joy and sorrow, symbolized that Daeryun pride.

> Mount Taebaek rises high
> the Nakdong River flows far
> Hand in hand came the agents of the coming age.
> With lofty ideals and steadfast will
> Let us go forth—let us go forth with the light
> we gained here become the morning star
> shining across every valley of this land.

We sang the school song—lyrics by Lee Sang-hwa and music by Kim Ho-ryong—at the top of our lungs, and the memories of training our bodies and minds while sweating on the Suseong plains are unforgettable. We made a firm resolution to become the morning stars, the vanguard of the coming century.

I had a strong interest in science. Under the guidance of teachers Lee Man-jeong and Jang Gi-jin, who taught chemistry and biology, students with a passion for science came together to form a science research club. Among them were Kim Dong-seong and Jeon Sang-yeol. The three of us were known at school as the "three musketeers of science." Kim Dong-seong later retired as a high school principal, and Jeon Sang-yeol became the president of an electric company.

The Three Musketeers' Chlorella Research
(From left: Jeon Sang-yeol, The Author, Kim Dong-seong)

In the fall of 1961, there was a national science exhibition at Gyeongbokgung Palace. Our science club, the "three musketeers," entered the exhibition with our research on "Chlorella," which received high praise as a creative project. We gained great popularity and won the Excellence Award. After the exhibition, we walked from Gyeongbokgung Palace to Dongdaemun, singing our school anthem along the way. As we toured the streets of Seoul, we proudly expressed Daeryun's spirit of excellence.

After that, Daeryun School prospered each year, achieving remarkable growth with the best facilities and the most prime location in Daegu. As Daegu's Suseong District developed into a new city, similar to Seoul's Gangnam, it became one of the top educational districts in the city. A benefactor from our alumni who worked in the construction industry modernized the school's facilities. Daeryun School became the top school in the country, consistently producing the highest number of Seoul National University admittees and top scorers in the college entrance exam. As a result, the pride and self-esteem of being a Daeryun alumnus grew even greater.

3. Junk Boots from the Yankee Market

When I attended Daeryun School, I bought used military boots sold at the "Yankee Market" and wore them. These boots were durable and didn't require much maintenance, so I didn't have to worry about shoes for a long time. My friends even gave me the nickname "junk boots" because I wore these heavy boots for six years. They would follow me around, teasing me with "junk boots! junk boots!" Even now, when I attend alumni gatherings, the story of my "junk boots" still comes up and becomes the highlight of the conversation.

Yankee Market in Daeguv

At the time, Korea was recovering from the aftermath of the Korean War, and everyone was struggling in a world turned to ashes. Military supplies were abundant in the markets. Specifically, if you went to the alley near Daegu Station, you could find all sorts of American-made goods and military items. This place was called "Yankee Market" by the locals. During the war, items such as boots, uniforms, and mess kits were scavenged from corpses, and these durable and sturdy second-hand military products could be purchased for a very low price. Not only boots, but also old military uniforms could be bought, dyed black, and worn as a full outfit, which solved all my clothing needs. The inexpensive, durable, and easily usable second-hand military goods I relied on during my school years can be seen as a contributing factor to my later decision to pursue a career in the military.

I covered my tuition fees with scholarships, but living expenses were always tight, so I had to live a frugal lifestyle. I had never used a brand-new textbook. There were many places in the alleys of Daegu's Yankee Market and Banwoldang where you could buy second-hand textbooks, and I always searched for old bookstores to purchase used books for my studies. When the new semester began, poor students would flock to Yankee Market to find used books, taking notes on the author, publisher, and publication year, since they could only get books passed down from seniors or second-hand ones. When I happened to find the book I was looking for in relatively good condition, I felt like I had found a treasure. After buying such used books, I would tear up old calendars to make book covers, write the title on the cover with a magic marker, and then my preparations for the semester were complete.

During my middle and high school years, I only used second-hand military boots, old clothes, and second-hand books, which led to an unwelcome gift. I contracted tuberculosis, which was transmitted through the used items. During a group health check at school, I was diagnosed with tuberculosis. Since I was living alone and wasn't eating well, using only second-hand items contributed to the tuberculosis being transmitted to my body. My teacher informed me about the health center, so I went to the health center in Suseong-dong, Daegu. At that time, there were many tuberculosis patients in Korea, and the World Health Organization sent a large amount of tuberculosis medication. After taking an X-ray and undergoing a health check, the health center gave me tuberculosis medicine called "Pas-zid" for free.

When the vacation came and I went home, my mother, feeling sorry that she couldn't feed me well during the regular days, would prepare all kinds of delicious food for me. In particular, she would catch a bullfrog, which was said to be good for tuberculosis, and make bullfrog soup every day. Thanks to the medication from the health center and my mother's loving care, my tuberculosis was completely cured. However, when I entered the military academy and had an annual health checkup, a scar always appeared on the chest X-ray. Each time I had a health checkup, I had to undergo a secondary, detailed examination and receive a final verdict that there was no problem, which was quite a hassle.

After my tuberculosis was cured, I moved into the Yookyeong Dormitory in Dongin-dong, Daegu, with my high school classmate, Cho Myeong-rae. A philanthropist had rented a Japanese-style house from the government during the Japanese colonial era and was running a charitable project to help students who were struggling to study. At Yookyeong Dormitory, I met senior Song Dae-heon. Two years older than me, Senior Song treated me like a younger brother. Later, he entered the 22nd class of the Military Academy and, while serving in the military, became a close benefactor and a guiding figure for my life's path.

The Yookyeong Dormitory only admitted students who were recommended by their schools for their academic excellence, so everyone there was a top student and a model pupil. The living expenses were low, and the atmosphere was great for studying. The dormitory director, an elderly and kind-hearted person, not only gave us life lessons to guide us on the right path but also took great care to ensure that we had no inconveniences in our daily lives.

Yookyeong Dormitory

The dormitory director had a daughter. When studying, I would sometimes hear her playing the piano, and instead of focusing on my work, I would find myself distracted by her, which was a clear sign that puberty had arrived. However, these daydreams were nothing more than a distant fantasy. The pressing goal of entering the military academy left me with neither the mental nor the time to pursue such distractions. Next to the dormitory, there was a bakery. Early in the morning, after washing my face with cold water, I would sit down to study, but the smell of freshly baked bread would waft into my room, making it hard to concentrate. With my stomach growling, I would desperately wish for just one bite of that bread. Yet, with my tight living expenses, I never got the chance to taste that bread, and I had to finish my time at the dormitory without ever having had it.

At this time, I received scholarships not only from Daeryun School but also from the Rotary Club. The Daegu Education Office had selected exemplary students who performed well academically and recommended them as scholarship candidates to the Rotary Club. When I went to the Rotary Club's breakfast meeting to receive the scholarship, all the people gathered there were middle-aged gentlemen with white hair. These distinguished individuals were intellectuals with noble character, invited to listen to breakfast lectures by well-known personalities. As I received the scholarship, I made a resolution to help people in difficult circumstances, just like these individuals, and I continued to receive the valuable scholarship regularly, studying diligently.

4. Years of Turmoil

Shortly after entering Daeryun High School in 1960, I witnessed the 4.19 Revolution. The 4.19 Student Revolution had its roots in Daegu. The long-standing dictatorship of Syngman Rhee and the Liberty Party sought to maintain power by suppressing the opposition and using corrupt methods to re-elect Rhee and his vice president, Lee Ki-bung. The opposition Democratic Party's presidential candidate, Dr. Jo Byeong-ok, was scheduled to hold a rally in Daegu on Sunday, February 28, 1960. However, the ruling party, in an effort to prevent people from gathering at the opposition's rally, ordered all elementary, middle, and high school students in Daegu to attend school, even though it was a Sunday.

Student protesters on April 19

Outraged by the actions of the ruling Liberty Party, we protested, shouting "Do not use students for politics," while carrying our school bags. The graduation ceremony of Daeryun Middle School on March 7, 1960, was also disrupted by our political discontent. This act served as a catalyst, leading to demonstrations across the country. Ultimately, the 4.19 Revolution was ignited, bringing an end to Syngman Rhee's 12-year rule and his attempts at perpetual power. After the collapse of the Rhee regime, the transitional government of Heo Jeong took over to prepare for a new republic. However, under an unstable political environment, the weak transitional government only exacerbated social chaos. In the midst of the deteriorating atmosphere where the spirit of the 4.19 Revolution seemed to be fading, military elites, including General Park Chung-hee, were deeply concerned about the future of the country.

When I entered my second year at Daeryun High School, General Park Chung-hee, along with the 8th class of the Korea Military Academy, led the 5.16 Military Coup. On the early morning of May 16, Colonel Park Chung-hee, who was the deputy commander of the 2nd Army, crossed the Han River with about 250 officers and 3,500 soldiers, and occupied key institutions in Seoul. He established the Military Revolutionary Committee and took full control, launching the Third Republic. While the 5.16 Military Coup was politically undemocratic, it became a turning point in history for the modernization of the country.

For our nation, which had been forced to endure a history of suffering and disgrace due to the lack of an independent and self-reliant system, the determination to modernize the country was made and put into action. Our people cut their hair to make wigs and sold them abroad. In every neighborhood, taffy sellers were mobilized to shout, "Sell your hair! Sell your hair!" They collected the long, braided hair of women. Rural mothers cut their hair to send their sons to school in Seoul, or to buy rice to survive. This led to the development of the wig industry in Korea.

They made beautiful flowers out of cheap plastic and sold them abroad. They made teddy bears and sold them abroad. A nationwide rat-catching campaign was launched. They made so-called "Korean mink" from rat fur and sold it abroad. Anything that could make money was made and sold abroad. In this way, in 1965, Korea achieved a $100 million export. The world was astonished. "Did those beggars export $100 million?" The world looked at us with amazement, calling it the "Miracle on the Han River."[2]

---

2   Jo Wang-ho, *Modern Korean History for Youth* (Duri Media, 2006), pp. 201–205.

5.16 Military Coup and the modernization of Korea

The reason we were able to host the Olympics and the World Cup and make the world recognize South Korea as a powerful nation was due to the hard work of miners and nurses dispatched to West Germany, as well as the soldiers who fought in the Vietnam War. The miners who worked in the deep coal mines, the nurses, the soldiers who shed their blood on foreign battlefields, and the laborers who worked in the scorching desert construction sites of the Middle East—all of their blood, sweat, and tears made today's prosperous South Korea possible. Through the tumultuous years marked by the 4.19 Revolution, the 5.16 Military Coup, the 10.26 Assassination, the 12.12 Military Insurrection, and eventually the 6.10 Struggle, South Korea achieved industrialization, democratization, and informatization, becoming a country that stretches out to the world. A developed nation is not built for free; it is made through the noble blood and sweat of our people.

5. The Spirit of Martial Arts Cultivated in the Judo Hall

While the 5.16 Military Coup took place and South Korea was on its way to modernization, I was focusing on my studies. Although I worked hard on my academics, I was also very interested in martial arts. I joined the judo club at Daeryun School and spent my free time dedicating myself to both physical and mental training. Judo requires a level of discipline and strict regulations that is unmatched by any other sport. It is not just about refining techniques or building physical strength, but also about developing one's character and embodying the virtue of self-sacrifice. That is why judo is not called a sport, but a "do".

When practicing judo, you had to strip off all your underwear and wear a gi. In winter, changing into the gi was the most painful part. Putting on the cold gi made you feel a chill at first. After practicing falling techniques a few times on the mat, only then would you begin to sweat and be in the proper condition for training. Once your body loosened up, you would neatly tie your belt, bow to your partner respectfully, and then begin training. One unforgettable memory from my judo days was when our Daeryun Judo team won first place at the 8th Gyeongbuk Sports Festival. I will never forget Kim Pan-oh, the passionate coach who led our team with great enthusiasm. After graduating from university, he became the judo teacher at Daeryun School and taught us by directly sparring with us. After school ended, he was already in his gi, waiting for us. While teaching us judo was important, he also led by example, showing us what it truly meant to live the way of the "do."

Immediately after the Korean War, most classrooms were used for military mobilization, so only a few facilities were available. Due to a lack of facilities, the school foundation built a new hall that could also serve as a gymnasium, which allowed it to be used as a judo gymnasium. Thanks to the good judo facilities, we were able to participate in various competitions and even win first place.

The martial spirit trained under the guidance of teacher Kim Pan-oh became the motivation for me to attend the military academy. Judo and martial arts are connected in many ways.

While being a scholar is good, it was even more important to study while also practicing martial arts, as this cultivated true leadership with both literary and martial skills. The leadership I developed through judo at Daeryun School became a great catalyst for me to unleash my potential as a national asset at the Korea Military Academy. The foundation I built in high school through judo was a great help in continuing to practice martial arts at the academy. Having attained the ranks of 2nd Dan in judo, 1st Dan in keomdo, and 5th Dan in hapkido, my martial arts skills became a strong pillar for me throughout my life as a martial artist.

The Daeryun Judo Club win at the 8th Gyeongbuk Sports Festival
(I am standing first from the left in the back row)

Another reason I decided to apply to the military academy

was the recognition, gained through experiencing the Korean War, that a strong national power is needed to overcome the tragedies of war. While there are many elements that make up national power, no one could argue that national defense is the most fundamental element. The tragic defeat we suffered at the hands of neighboring countries such as Japan and China during the late Joseon Dynasty, which ultimately led to 36 years of Japanese colonial rule, was due to the weakness of our national defense. During the Korean War, I had to give up half of the school grounds to the military and study in the remaining half, surrounded by barbed wire. I would sit under a tall Himalayan cedar tree in one corner of the playground, lost in deep contemplation.

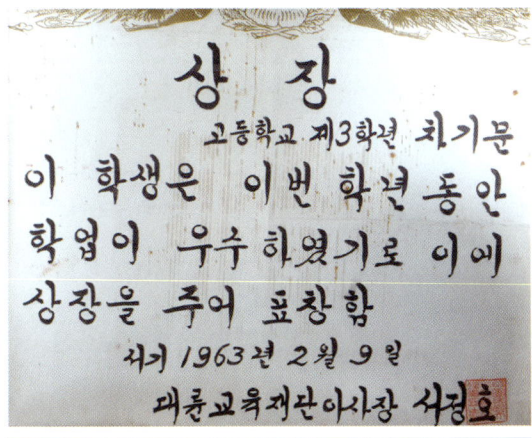

The Daeryun Foundation Chairman's Award

As I had received the honorary title of Chairman of the Daeryun Foundation, I pondered my future career. I thought about how there should never again be a tragedy like the Korean War on this land, and decided to become a national asset. Remembering the famous saying, "If you want peace, prepare for war," I resolved to become a strong pillar for my country and knocked on the doors of the Korea Military Academy.

Chapter 3

| The Immortal Spirit of the Hwarang |

1. My First Step into the Hwarangdae

My parents, who had directly experienced the Pacific War and the Korean War, opposed my decision to go to the military academy. Having known only that going to the military meant certain death, my father and mother couldn't understand why I wanted to attend the military academy. It took considerable time to help them understand what a military academy was. At that time, the Korea Military Academy was so popular that private institutes were even established to prepare for its entrance exams. Despite the fierce competition, I was confident I would pass, having been the top student at Daeryun for six years. Not knowing which academy was the best, I decided to apply to all three: the Korea Military Academy, the Naval Academy, and the Air Force Academy.

Upon reviewing the admission guidelines, I found that the

Korea Military Academy and the Air Force Academy had their exams on the same date, while the Naval Academy had its exam on a different day. So, I applied to both the Korea Military Academy and the Naval Academy and took the exams. Since the military academy exams were special exams, they were held before other university exams. The process for the Korea Military Academy exam was complicated. Even if I passed the first round, the second round of interviews and physical tests were rigorous. After passing the first round with excellent results, the examiner asked me a question during the second round interview.

"Why did you apply to the Korea Military Academy?"

"I applied to walk the eternal path of justice rather than the easy path of momentary comfort."

"Being a soldier is a difficult profession that requires placing honor above money and sacrificing oneself for the country and people, rather than seeking personal wealth and fame. Do you still want to pursue a career as a soldier?"

"Yes! I believe that the path of a soldier, who dedicates himself to the country and people rather than personal gain, aligns with my life philosophy and character."

I could sense from the interviewer's expression that my

confident answer was well received. To enter the Korea Military Academy, physical strength was emphasized above all else. The physical fitness test was conducted over two days. No matter how outstanding one's academic performance was, if their physical condition was weak, they could not pass. To pass the physical test, the following requirements had to be met: a grenade throw of at least 30 meters, a 2,000-meter run in under 9 minutes 30 seconds, a 100-meter run in under 16 seconds, at least 4 pull-ups, and lifting 35kg at least twice.

I stayed at a guesthouse near Taereung while undergoing the physical fitness test, and the landlady, who took care of the examinees every year, specially managed my meals. She prepared light yet nutritious food and constantly encouraged me to do well on the test. In the guesthouse, there were many students from other regions. One of the people who shared the same room with me was Noh Dong-jun, a student from Busan Haedong High School who spoke in the Gyeongsang dialect. He also passed the test alongside me, and we became close friends.

The result was that I was accepted to both the Korea Military Academy and the Naval Academy. I was ranked 27th out of 244 accepted at the Korea Military Academy, and 9th out of 102 accepted at the Naval Academy.

The Korea Military Academy's second round of exams

The Naval Academy announced the final results first, and even issued an order for the entry date before the Korea Military Academy announced its acceptance list. This was a measure to prevent those who were accepted to both from choosing the Korea Military Academy over the Naval Academy. In response, the Korea Military Academy also took action. As I was on my way to Jinhae to enter the Naval Academy, they announced the list of successful candidates over the radio.

Successful Applicants to the 23rd Class of the Korea Military Academy by High School

High School	Number of successful applicants	Name
Seoul High School	15	Song Su-seop, Jeong Ji-yong, Kim Mun-so, Kwak Yun-geun, Lee Jeong-hwan, Park No-cheol, Hong Jeong-heon, Yu Gwan-hui, Park Yong-seung, Jang U-gyun, Kim Chang-hak, Kim Pung-gu, Park Yeong-il, Kim Byeong-seop, Lee Hong-ju
Gwangju High School	13	Mun Il-seop, Kim U-yeol, Park Chang-su, Cha Yeong-seop, Jeon Sang-yeol, Kim Yeong-geol, Jang Dong-uk, Choi Gi-chang, Park Seong-il, Jang Ji-mun, Lee Geon-bu, Kim Yong-ung, Kim Yeong-mok
Busan High School	12	Kwon Yeong-hyo, Lee Seong-hui, Song Yeong-jun, Oh Jun-hong, Kim Jeong-won, Heo Jin-yeong, Seo Si-u, Park Bang-ung, Min Wan-gi, Lee Deok-gwan, Park Seung-bu, Jo Yeong-hwi
Jinju High School	9	Yu Do-hyeon, Kim Geon-il, Hwang Il-hun, Park Ho-gil, Son Mun-seong, Jeong Hwa-eon, Jeong Hyeon-ryang, Yun Jung-yeong, Lee Jong-gyu
Daejeon High School	8	Im Yeong-hwan, Nam Gi-heon, Lee Chun-ung, U Jong-il, Oh Yeong-gwan, Park Jong-gyu, Gil Yeong-cheol, Gwon O-seong
Gyeongnam High School	8	Choi Chung-nam, Hong Yong-chan, Kim Sang-won, Yang Sang-jin, An Seong-yong, Kim Dong-yun, Choi Byeong-won, Kim Seong-gyu
Gwangju II High School	8	Park Ju-yeong, Jeong Wan-chae, Park Jeong-cheol, Kim Yong-gu, U Hyeong-sik, Park Jeong-seok, Park Hye-cheol, Heo Gi-ung
Gyeongdong High School	7	Gu Ja-yeol, Heo Yeol, Park Hui-bok, Lee Jeong-nam, Yun Bong-sik, Park Eung-ik, Sin Un-cheol
Seongnam High School	6	Yu Seung-u, Jang Gwang-nam, Sim Gi-seop, Lee Jong-wan, An Heung-yang, No Bu-ryung

Gyeongbuk High School	5	Jeong Myeong-hwa, Min Seong-gi, U Yeong-mu, Kim Dong-mun, Kim Ho-gwon
Masan High School	5	Seol Yeong-gil, Go Yong-il, Kim Chang-gil, Gwon Cheol-ho, Kim Hak-yeong
Gyotong High School	5	Park Yeong-ik, Choi Yeong-bu, Kim Yeong-ri, Yun Sang-yeong, Kim Ju-myeong
Kyungpook National University High School	5	Jeong Jeong-taek, Gwon Dae-po, Heo Cheol, Ha Jeong-gon, Kim Gwang-su
Whimoon High School	5	Kim Mun-hwan, Kim Hwang, Sin Gwang-chi, Kim Jung-seo, Won Gi-ho
Jeonju High School	5	Kim Myeong-se, Yang Gil-yong, No Si-deok, Lee Nam-sin, Yu Yeong-gil
Yongsan High School	5	Lee Yeong-il, Yun Hyeong-tae, Lee Je-won, Park Seong-tae, Lee Chung-nam
Jemulpo High School	5	Kim Jeong-ho, Lee Jong-seon, Kim Chan-sik, Yun Yong-seop, Kim Eun-gyeom
Namseong High School	4	Kim Dae-hun, Seo Geo-ung, Jeong Bok-seop, Song O-seop
Cheongju High School	4	Jeong Gi-jun, Choi Gi-ok, Sin Dong-pil, Kim Seong-yong
Kyungbok High School	4	Sin Gwang-gyun, Mun Jong-yun, Jeon Gwan, Mun Dong-myeong
Boseong High School	4	Yu Je-hyeon, Kang Jong-pil, Kwak Won-mun, Choi Jong-seon
Chosun University High School	4	Kim Tae-eon, No Nam-seop, Jeong Byeong-tae, Choi Su-mok
Gyeongju High School	3	Son Su-tae, Choi In-hwan, Lee Mun-won

Daekwang High School	3	Na Gi-san, Kim Gwon-hu, Lee Yeong-geun
Seongdong High School	3	Yang Yeong-bu, Lee Yeong-sik, Kim In-geol
Yeosu High School	3	Park Jeong-cheol, Jeong Gi-ho, Bae Ui-ung
Commercial High Schools	10	Kim Yeong-gu (Masan), Kang Seong-nam (Masan), Jo Hyo-nam (Daegyeong), Kim Mun-gi (Gangneung), Seo Gu-ung (Daegu), Jeong Yeong-jin (Daegu), Jo Ui-ung (Daegu), Kang Seung-gil (Daedong), Yang Yeong-gi (Jeju), Mun Chang-hun (Jeju)
Agricultural High Schools	9	An Seong-cheong (Uljin), Lee Won-rak (Jinju), Gwon Jeong-haeng (Jinju), Lee Sang-do (Uiryeong), Han Jeong-ju (Goheung), Lee Geum-saeng (Sacheon), Lee Seong-u (Wonju), Lee Yeong-gil (Namhae), Kim Mal-deuk (Ulsan)
High Schools of Education	7	On Chang-il (Jeonju), Park Jeong-ung (Gwangju), Sin Hyeon-su (Chungju), Lee Bu-jik (Andong), Ban Won-jung (Andong), Kim Gu-ung (Gunsan), Jang Geun-sik (Daejeon)
Technical High Schools	5	Kim Gang-hwang (Busan), Kim Hak (Busan), Kim Yong-gyeong (Gwangju), Jang Gil-nam (Yeongwol), Han Gwang-so (Mokpo)
Osan High School	2	Lee Jae, Hong Bong-gil
Muntae High School	2	Mun Jun-yeong, Kim Gil-sam
Dongnae High School	2	Yu Han-ju, Jo Yeong-sin
Jungang High School	2	Ju Seon-man, Nam Sang-uk
Gimcheon High School	2	Gu Il-cheol, Kim Sang-deok

Donga High School	2	Kim Hyeon-su, Jeong Jeong-sang
Sejong High School	2	An Jun-bu, Im Jeong-sun
Gyesung High School	2	Park Yeong-gi, Seo Se-ho
SNU High School of Education	2	Seo Chung-il, Kim Jae-ik
Marine High School	2	Lee Yeong-eon (Mokpo), Jeong Jin-won (Busan)
Others	26	Sin Hyeong-gang (Gyeonggi), Park Seung-il (Baejae), Cha Kimoon (Daeryun), Kim Seon-tae (Suwon), Lee Jong-gyu (Dae) (Yeongnam), Hong Seong-won (Dongseong), Jo Tae-hyeong (Jecheon), Kim Seok-jae (Anui), Jeon Su-jin (Incheon), Lee Jae-hwan (Wando Fisheries), Jang Pan-yong (Salesio), No Dong-jun (Haedong), Choi Jeong-ung (Jinhae), Park No-yang (Seonggwang), Lee Jeong-gyun (Chuncheon), In Seong-gyeong (Hapdeok), Park Hyeon-gyu (Gangmun), Choi Jae-rim (Daeseong), Park Yeong-taek (Hanseong), Oh Ju-ui (Dongbuk), Lee Ho-mu (Inchang), Kim Yeong-won (Ohyeon), Kim Geon-seop (Gogye), Im Ho-gwon (Hongseong), Song Yeong-geol (Heungguk), Kim Il-ung (GED)

Source: Biographies of the Korea Military Academy 23rd Class, 1997, p. 25.

On my way down to Jinhae, I returned to Daegu to meet with my teachers and seniors to ask where I should go. I found myself in the fortunate position of having to make a happy decision. Vice Principal Choi Yu-ryeon cited the proverb, "Horses should be sent to Jeju, and people should be sent to Seoul," and recommended that I choose the Korea Military Academy in Seoul. Others also advised me to join the Army, saying that our military was still primarily centered on the Army and that it would be better to go where the organization was larger. Based on the advice of my teachers and seniors, I decided to enter the Korea Military Academy.

When the total of 244 successful applicants was broken down by region, the numbers were as follows: Seoul: 105, Gyeongnam: 51, Gyeongbuk: 25, Jeonnam: 37, Jeonbuk: 7, Chungnam: 10, Chungbuk: 4, Gangwon: 1, and Jeju: 4. At that time, if one had the academic qualifications to be accepted into the Korea Military Academy, it was said that getting into Seoul National University would have been relatively easy. In order to increase the university admission rate, the teachers encouraged me to also apply to the College of Engineering at Seoul National University. However, since the admission notice from the Korea Military Academy arrived early, I had no choice but to head to Taereung, where the Academy was located, in order to begin training.

Among the students who entered the Korea Military Academy as part of the 23rd class, many had previously attended regular universities. There were even some who had transferred after attending the Naval and Air Force Academies. Since most had repeated 2~3 years before being accepted, the average age of the 23rd class was higher compared to other classes. The Korea Military Academy assigns cadet numbers based on entrance exam rankings, and since I was ranked 27th, I was given the cadet number 2,694. This meant that I was the 2,694th person to be accepted since the founding of the Korea Military Academy.

2. Human Transformation: Basic Military Training

"Toot-toot, da ~ toot-toot, da ~ toot-toot-toot-toot ~ toot-toot, da~"

"Gather in order of arrival within 3 minutes!"

"One! Two! Three!..."

"Those in positions 3 and below, circle around the far independent post and gather again in order of arrival!"

"You haven't even properly tied your boots!"

"Where's your helmet?"

At 06:00 sharp! It was still so dark outside that nothing could be seen, but with the loud sound of the reveille, the commanding voices of the tiger-like cadet leaders rang out. With the start of induction, basic military training began. This basic training is called "Beast Training," meaning training where you're treated not as a person, but as an animal.

After induction, I got my hair shaved short and received a military uniform and personal rifle for the first time. The rookies, still unsure of how to properly tie their bootlaces, began their military life with a "first-come, first-served" approach. Every action started and ended in a race to be first. The "first-come, first-served" method meant that everyone ran to a designated goal and then returned, with the last person being cut from the line in order, starting from the first. Those who were cut had to choose another goal and keep running. If you didn't run fast enough to be first, you had to keep running until there was only one person left. The cadets, out of breath from the relentless sprints, shouted the fourth verse of the national anthem and the cadet creed loudly as part of the drill.

Induction is a one-month basic military training period that teaches the fundamental attitude required to be a cadet before officially joining the academy. It is a process of purging worldly habits, both physically and mentally, and transforming into a cadet. This period instills the correct posture for being a cadet, internalizes the rules of dormitory life, military etiquette, and the basic attitudes of a soldier, making it the time when most people drop out. The cadet leaders, selected from the 4th-year cadets, were the ones who carried out the basic military training for us, the rookies. The cadet leaders who were in charge of training us were even more fearsome than tigers.

The Creed of a Cadet

1. We dedicate our lives to the nation and the people.
2. We live always within the bounds of honor and faith.
3. We choose the difficult path of justice over the comfortable path of injustice.

"You are assigned to 3rd Company, 2nd Platoon, 1st Squad!"

Each of us was assigned to our respective unit formations. This designation represented the community in which each cadet would live, sleep, eat, and run together. Cadets had to march in a straight line and eat in a strict manner. No matter how little time there was, walking in curves was not allowed. During meals, some new cadets, still unfamiliar with the system, would spill rice or soup. When this happened, the entire group would be punished together. This was a way of instilling a sense of unity and collective responsibility. After a day of the exhausting "first-come, first-served" routine, hunger would strike. No matter how much was eaten, the hunger seemed to return quickly. During this time, the appetite was so strong that one could almost digest steel.

Induction and basic military training

Once, during meal time, while saying a prayer of gratitude, Cadet K took a spoonful of Cadet P's food and placed it into his own bowl. After finishing the prayer and opening his eyes, Cadet P noticed that a spoonful of his food was missing, which led to a confrontation between him and Cadet K. As a result of this incident, the entire group was unable to eat and had to go to the training ground, where they received "race-order" punishment for the entire day.

Another time, there was one piece of kimchi left in the side dish bowl, and both Cadet M and Cadet C simultaneously tried to pick it up with their forks. They both insisted that it was theirs, leading to a fight. Once again, we were not allowed to eat and had to undergo collective punishment. During the Beast Training period, not only our bodies but also our minds were being transformed, becoming more animalistic by instinct.

At 10 p.m., a roll call is conducted. To attend roll call, personal belongings must be organized, and the room must be thoroughly cleaned. If the rifle is improperly cleaned or even a speck of dust is found during roll call, punishment will be enforced throughout the night. Roll call is to ensure that both individuals and their belongings are in their proper places and that all items are in usable condition. When standing at attention at the edge of the bed, the 4th year cadet leaders would approach, and automatically, the room would be filled with the loud recitation of the individual's name and rank.

"Cadet?"

"Yes! Cadet 2698! Kim Mal-deuk."

"Cadet?"

"Yes! Cadet 2722! Kwon Dae-po."

"Cadet?"

"Yes! Cadet 2743! Yoon Joong-ryeong."

"You are a higher rank than me, a lieutenant colonel..."

(*Lieutenant colonel in Korean is also pronounced Joong-ryeong*)

The unusual names and the cadet leaders' joking remarks made it impossible for everyone to hold back their laughter. Eventually, one cadet burst out laughing, and soon everyone was laughing uncontrollably. As a result, all of us had to wear full gear and break the ice in a cold pond, where we received group punishment all night long.

After the evening roll call, we reflected on our day by writing in our diaries. There was a time limit for writing, and as we held our pencils and tried to recall the events of the day, the command "Cease all movement!" would echo through the room. Everything was so mechanically regimented that there was no time to think. Some cadets, unable to endure this process, attempted to desert. Cadets who tried to escape by climbing over the barbed wire were caught by the military police and expelled.

The day, which passed like lightning, came to an end, and with the sound of the taps for sleep, I shoved my heavy body into the bed. The sound of dogs barking in the quiet Taereung valley turned into a yearning for home, which made my heart ache even more. The sound of a train whistle echoed across the silent night sky. The thought that I could return home if I boarded that train made me tear up as I drifted into sleep.

On weekends, we were able to take a break. Emphasizing the importance of working hard when necessary and playing hard when the time came, we were allowed to visit the church, cathedral, or temple on Sundays, all located within the school grounds. While family visits were prohibited, group meals were allowed, so we bought bread and drinks to share as a group. I never realized how delicious steaming hot gyombo bread, red bean bread, and small rice cakes could be. The mountain of bread would disappear in no time. Once, during bread distribution, the duty cadet slyly slipped a rice cake into his mouth, which was discovered, and as a result, we all received group punishment from the cadet leaders throughout the holiday.

Company Formation Chart

Companies	Cadets
1st Company (28 cadets)	Choi Chung-nam, Shin Hyung-gang, Moon Il-seop, Moon Jun-young, Jeong Jeong-taek, Kim Myung-se, Kim Yeong-gu, Kim Chang-gil, Lee Yeong-sik, Choi Gi-ok, Lee Jae-hwan, Woo Yeong-mu, Shin Gwang-chi, Jang Dong-wook, Gwak Won-mun, Kim Eun-gyeom, Choi Jae-rim, Park Hui-bok, Jeong Hyeon-ryang, Park Seong-tae, Park Yeong-gi, Jo Ui-woong, Lee Jong-wan, Won Gi-ho, Kim Seong-yong, Gil Yeong-cheol, Lee Chung-nam, Choi Su-mok

2nd Company (28 cadets)	Lim Yeong-hwan, Jeong Ji-yong, Ko Yong-il, Na Gi-san, Kim Gwon-hu, Park Chang-su, Yoo Do-hyeon, Lee Yeong-il, Hwang Il-hun, Heo Gi-woong, Heo Yeol, Yun Hyeong-tae, Kim Yeong-geol, Woo Hyeong-sik, Han Jeong-ju, Seo Geo-woong, Park Yeong-taek, Kim Jae-ik, Kim Yeong-won, Choi Byeong-won, Park Jong-gyu, Jeong Yeong-jin, Kim Chang-hak, Ha Jeong-gon, An Hong-yang, Kim In-geol, Jeong Jeong-sang, Kim Gwang-su
3rd Company (29 cadets)	Yu Je-hyeon, Song Su-seop, Kim Mun-so, Cha Kimoon, Joo Seon-man, Kim Jeong-ho, Jang Gwang-nam, Kim Gil-sam, Kim Sang-won, Jeon Gwan, Park Jeong-cheol, Kim Yong-gu, Sim Gi-seop, Jo Hyo-nam, Yun Jun-yeong, Yang Gil-yong, Yu Gwang-hee, Park Seong-il, An Jun-bu, Shin Dong-pil, Im Jeong-sun, Lee Jong-gyu, Lee Yeong-geun, Kim Pung-gu, Ban Won-jung, Park Yeong-il, Seo Se-o, Yu Yeong-gil, Jo Yeong-hwi
4th Company (30 cadets)	Lee Jae, Kwon Yeong-hyo, Park Ju-yeong, Song Yeong-jun, Kim Seok-jae, Kwon Dae-po, Seo Chung-il, Lee Jong-seon, Lee Bu-jik, Park Jeong-cheol, Kim Hwang, Lee Sang-do, Cha Yeong-seop, Kim Dong-yun, Kim Hyeon-su, Lee Jeong-gyun, Kim Yong-gyeong, Kang Seung-gil, Noh Si-deok, Jang Woo-gyun, Kim Hak, Song Yeong-geol, Kim Mal-deuk, Yun Yong-seop, Kim Ho-gwon, Lee Deok-gwan, Lee Seong-woo, Noh Bu-ryung, Kim Yeong-bok, Kim Byeong-seop
5th Company (29 cadets)	Son Su-tae, Hong Yong-chan, Kim Tae-eon, Park Seung-il, Lee Jong-gyu, Shin Gwang-gyun, Kim Gang-hwang, Lee Mun-won, Hong Bong-gil, Yang Sang-jin, Park Jeong-ung, Gu Il-cheol, Kim Jeong-won, Lee Won-rak, Jeon Sang-yeol, Jeong Hwa-eon, Hong Jeong-heon, Moon Dong-myeong, Choi Yeong-bu, Oh Ju-ui, Choi Gi-chang, Jeong Bok-seop, Kim Jin-seop, Park Hye-cheol, Park Seung-bu, Kim Mun-gi, Lee Yeong-eon, Park Eung-ik, Jeong Jin-won
6th Company (32 cadets)	Jeong Myeong-hwa, Min Seong-gi, Yoo Seung-woo, Choi In-hwan, Kim Woo-yeol, Hong Seong-won, Yoo Han-ju, Kim Mun-hwan, Kim Dae-hoon, Yang Yeong-bu, Shin Hyeon-su, Heo Cheol, Woo Jong-il, Lee Jeong-hwan, Lee Hong-ju, Kim Joong-seo, Park No-yang, Park Bang-ung, Jeong Gi-ho, Choi Jong-seon, Moon Chang-hoon, Kim Sang-deok, Kwon Jeong-haeng, Jo Yeong-shin, Lee Jin-bu, Lee Nam-shin, Kwon Cheol-ho, Shin Un-cheol, Song O-seop, Kim Ju-myeong, Kwon O-seong, Yang Chang-yeol

7th Company (30 cadets)	Kim Seon-tae, An Seong-cheong, On Chang-il, Noh Nam-seop, Park Yeong-ik, Nam Gi-heon, Moon Jong-yun, Jeon Su-jin, Lee Chung-woong, Kang Seong-nam, An Seong-yong, Heo Jin-yeong, Park No-cheol, Jang Pan-yong, Kim Gu-woong, Seo Gu-woong, Kim Dong-mun, Park Yong-seung, Lee Jeong-nam, Park Jeong-seok, Park Ho-gil, Jang Gil-nam, Kim Seong-gyu, Kim Yong-woong, Im Ho-geun, Han Gwang-so, Bae Ui-woong, Seo Se-ho, Jang Geun-sik, Park Chang-nam
8th Company (31 cadets)	Seol Yeong-gil, Lee Seong-hwi, Gu Ja-yeol, Jo Tae-hyeong, Oh Jun-hong, Kim Geon-il, Jeong Gi-jun, Jeong Wan-chae, Yang Yeong-gi, Kang Jong-pil, Gwak Yun-geun, Seo Si-woo, Son Mun-seong, Noh Dong-jun, Choi Jeong-woong, In Seong-gyeong, Oh Yeong-gwan, Park Hyeon-gyu, Min Wan-gi, Lee Geum-saeng, Kim Yeong-ri, I Je-weon, Jang Ji-mun, Kim Chan-sik, Kim Il-woong, Yun Bong-sik, Nam Sang-wook, Lee Ho-mu, Kim Hak-yeong, Lee Yeong-gil, Jeong Byeong-tae

Source: Biographies of the Korea Military Academy 23rd Class, 1997, p.19

On February 26, 1963, the graduation ceremony for the 19th class of the Korea Military Academy took place. The ceremony was held at Hwarang Parade Ground, with President Park Chung-hee in attendance, amid a snowstorm in extremely cold weather. We, the new cadets, also attended the ceremony in our combat uniforms to showcase the training we had undergone. In the freezing cold winter weather of minus 10°C, many cadets collapsed while standing rigidly in a tense posture. However, despite the freezing cold, we endured, fueled by the hope and expectation that we would officially move into the empty dormitory rooms vacated by the seniors.

3rd Company

I was assigned to the 3rd Company. The unit I belonged to as a cadet remained etched in my memory for life. In particular, the initial company assignment that began with basic military training was unforgettable. I believed that refraining from reorganizing units midway and maintaining consistent assignments would be better for preserving the memories of cadet life.

3. In the Crucible of Life

March 4, 1963!

Having successfully completed basic military training with the pursuit of young dreams in our hearts, we held the official entrance ceremony at the Hwarangdae Parade Ground, the hall of physical and mental discipline. At this ceremony, we took an oath to give our lives without hesitation for our country and people. A morale-boosting performance by female students from Seoul Arts High School, held to add brilliance to the cadet oath ceremony, lifted the spirits of the new cadets.

By donning the cadet uniform and participating in the official entrance ceremony, our formal life as cadets began. During the basic military training period, we were still cadet candidates and wore combat uniforms, but from this day forward, we were granted the status of cadets entitled to wear the neat and proper cadet uniform.

However, life in the cadet battalion was also a continuous stretch of grueling time. "0600 hours sharp!" As the reveille shattered the silence and pierced the dawn air, the tigers of Taereung Valley, still cloaked in darkness, began to roar. Before stars disappeared from the sky and even before the first light appeared in the east, we threw off our warm blankets and rushed out to the parade ground. Suppressing drowsy eyes and yawning mouths, we launched into the national anthem, The Way of the Soldier, the Cadet Creed, and a silent tribute to the patriotic forebears—thus began Hwarangdae's 25th hour.

Dress uniform

Duty uniform

Life at Hwarangdae was designed to cultivate cadets into elite officers of the military by fostering intellectual ability, noble character, mental fortitude, and a firm sense of national identity. Within this educational environment, cadets developed a spirit of cooperation, service, and sacrifice while enhancing their capacity for rational thinking and self-discipline. Under the guidance of outstanding training officers and excellent professors, they studied both general academics and military science and engaged in autonomous duty training to cultivate leadership and command capabilities.

There were honor systems in place to cultivate noble character, class association activities to encourage mutual refinement among classmates, and extracurricular activities and festivals to enrich emotional development and hobbies. Most daily life was spent within the cadet battalion, where tiger-like training officers guided us.

Cadet Cha Kimoon

Cadets at the Korea Military Academy set specific goals for each academic year. First-year cadets focus on instilling and internalizing discipline through collective spirit. Second-year cadets aim to develop a sense of duty, sacrifice, and service by practicing respect for rules and laws. Third-year cadets strive to foster initiative and a strong sense of professional responsibility as future officers. Fourth-year cadets concentrate on cultivating leadership and command abilities through rational leadership development.

A typical day in a cadet's life begins with the morning bugle call and roll call, followed by general academic classes conducted by the Academic Department. After classes, physical and martial arts training continues to strengthen both body and mind. Only after dinner are cadets given personal time for self-directed activities. During physical training hours, cadets may choose from various activities such as horseback riding, golf, swimming, taekwondo, judo, keomdo, soccer, and baseball.

I was a member of the judo team. After four years of training, I earned a second-degree black belt officially certified by the state upon graduation. Because I was at a fairly high level within the judo team, I represented the academy in national competitions. At the Seoul University Judo Tournament held on December 4, 1966, we won the championship.

Victory at the Seoul University Judo Tournament
(I am standing third from the left in the back row)

Every Monday, there was a formation ceremony followed by a 20 km group run. Since we had to run in full combat gear, some cadets would fall behind. It was always the same few who lagged behind. Group running was more about endurance than physical strength. One of the ways to cultivate endurance was precisely through this group run.

In the summer, cadets of each academic year received military training during the break. Various weapons courses and basic tactics were learned near the Hwarangdae in the first and second years.

"Drop and fire!"

"The target is the one ahead!"

"Fire!"

"Bang! Bang! Bang!"

"hit! hit!"

The life of a first-year cadet was so busy that there was hardly any time to blink. After completing the basic military training, I received my first letter. It was a letter from my nephew, Cha Seong-sook, and niece, Cha Seong-yeong, who lived in Daegu. There was no time to open the welcoming letter, and I could only read it when I went to the bathroom. During weekdays, I couldn't even think of writing a letter, and it was only on weekends that I could finally reply.

One of the rules that cadets at the Korea Military Academy must uphold is the system of honor. For cadets who regard honor as their life, this system allows them to take pride in themselves. The minimum standard of the honor system is not engaging in falsehoods, misconduct, or taking unfair advantages. All cadets must make it a habit to cultivate a sense of honor based on this minimum standard. When honor is violated, the cadet must report it to their conscience, and through conscience regulation, they are provided with an opportunity for reflection. When cadets feel guilty about violating their honor, they are required to voluntarily report to the honor committee directly or use the company report box to quickly submit a conscience report.

The enjoyable life as a cadet
(I am standing second person from the right in the back row.)

In the scorching heat of the midsummer's sweltering days, standing on the heated ground, I focused on aiming at the vitality of youth. Although it later became the national team athlete village, the Taereung field, which had once been a shooting range for cadets, was soaked in the sharp scent of sweat from combat uniforms. The hill, which had transformed into the Taereung Golf Course, was drenched in sweat from individual combat and squad tactics training, lasting until the sun set. In the hot weather, training with flamethrowers and chemical warfare gas chamber exercises became even more excruciating.

"Every drop of sweat shed during training saves a drop of blood in real combat."

With the instructor's shouting, training after training continued under the scorching July sky.

In the third year, cadets receive training by rotating through each branch school. Infantry, artillery, and armored training were conducted in Gwangju, communication in Daejeon, and engineering in Gimhae. The most grueling course was the guerilla training and tactical combined training at the Gwangju Infantry School. It was a process that combined the tactical education learned at Taereung during the first and second years. Internal life was also strict, and if points were accumulated, outings were prohibited. When the weekend came, the instructor would bring a stack of documents.

"If only there were a letter in here..."

"33 penalty points and 60 minutes of night marching?"

"Oh my god!"

Instead of the long-awaited letter, a penalty notice arrived, causing the cadets' shoulders to droop. The most anticipated outing was when they could go to downtown Gwangju, watch a movie, and stroll around Hwanggeum-dong, fully embracing the pride and self-respect of being a cadet. Cadets from Gwangju invited their classmates to their homes. Kim Yong-gu, whose home was in Gangjin, invited us to his house, where his family warmly welcomed us. Cadets share a bond of camaraderie as close as that of brothers, so their parents treat other cadets like their own children. Because of this bond, the Korea Military Academy classmates remain like family for life. The strong friendships and love become another treasure that others cannot have. When we entered the third year, the company formation was changed. This was to provide an opportunity to become closer with cadets from other companies.

In the fourth year, cadets were assigned to front-line units for platoon leader practice. With the role of a trainee platoon leader, they led real personnel, developing the qualities required to be a platoon leader after commissioning. They practiced all the situations that occur in a practical unit, including ambushes, reconnaissance, soldiers internal life, and unit management. They even extracted issues that needed improvement and wrote them down in small handwriting in a notebook. This was to serve as important reference material after being appointed as a platoon leader.

4. Army, Navy, and Air Force Cadets' Brotherhood Oath

In a small country like South Korea, it is more efficient for the army, navy, and air force to integrate. Joint operations are much more effective than independent operations by each branch. In large countries like the United States, the navy and air force operate independently overseas, but in a region like ours, which is only one theater, the army, navy, and air force must carry out integrated operations. For this reason, there have been many opinions suggesting that before forming an integrated military, the army, navy, and air force academies should first be unified. However, due to the conflicting interests of each branch, this has not been realized. It would be beneficial if, at least in the first and second years, cadets were integrated to receive common subject training, and from the third year, they could specialize at their respective service academies.

In this context, while living as a cadet at the Korea Military Academy, opportunities were provided to also interact with cadets from the Navy and Air Force academies. Through mutual exchange visits between the service academies, the bonds between cadets from different branches were strengthened. Navy and Air Force cadets visited the Korea Military Academy, and Korea Military Academy cadets visited the Navy and Air Force academies, where they learned naval and air force tactics, thereby forging a bond of brotherhood.

The KMA cadets are disassembling aircraft engines at the Air Force Academy.

When we went to the Naval Academy, we trained on a destroyer. Riding the destroyer and cutting through towering waves as we sailed into the open sea, I was able to understand how challenging the Navy can be. At the Air Force Academy, we had the opportunity to practice everything from operating fighter jet engines to the training process for pilots. Since I had studied mechanical engineering at the Korea Military Academy, disassembling and reassembling Air Force fighter jets was easy to understand.

The most memorable experience of cadet life was undoubtedly the sports festival of the Army, Navy, and Air Force academies. Every year, around October, coinciding with the National Armed Forces Day, the sports festival of the three military academies was held at the now-defunct Dongdaemun Stadium. The three-day event, which included soccer, rugby, and relay races, was also popular among the general public. The sports festival reached its peak during the cheering competition. While the athletes' skills were important, the entire student body devoted their full effort to practicing the cheers.

To prepare for the sports festival of the three military academies, as soon as summer vacation ended, we immediately began cheerleading practice. Every day, after the faculty classes, we gathered on the steps of Hwarang Parade Ground to practice under the guidance of the cheerleader. The lower-year cadets practiced without even going to the bathroom, enduring intense discipline. During this time, senior cadets serving in the front and rear areas would come to the school and encourage the younger cadets in every way possible, which made us forget our fatigue and focus entirely on cheering.

During the sports festival of the three military academies,

each academy had its own unique cheering competition. The Korea Military Academy was known for the "Mulaca" cheer, the Naval Academy for the "Penguin" cheer, and the Air Force Academy for the "Eagle" cheer. "Murka" was a cheer created by Lee Dong-hee, the 11th class cheerleader of the Korea Military Academy, where everyone would shout a loud, unified cheer, bringing the athletes and cheering cadets together as one. This cheer instilled a sense of pride and self-respect as eternal cadets of the Korea Military Academy.

"Mulac, Veni, Vidi, Vici

Eokseon M.A., Vital, Vigor

Kashkara, Leven, Lion Tiger

Caress Caress, Military Academy"

The "Murka" chant emphasizes not only the determined spirit of victory of the Korea Military Academy but also highlights the values of generosity and inclusiveness. It blends Korean, English, Latin, German, and Chinese characters. Analyzing the meaning of "Murka" reveals the following:

Mul-ac: A combination of the words "Military" and "Academy," symbolizing the strength of the military academy

Veni, Vidi, Vici: Latin phrase meaning "I came, I saw, I conquered," famously uttered by Julius Caesar after crossing the Rubicon, signaling a victorious achievement.

Eokseon M.A: A mix of Korean and English, representing the strong and resilient Korea Military Academy.

Vital, Vigor: English adjectives encapsulating endless vitality, energetic spirit, life force, and unyielding courage and determination.

Kashkara: A pure Korean phrase meaning "Go and defeat the enemy," symbolizing boldness and courage.

Leben: German word meaning "life," and in the context, it signifies the chivalric spirit of showing mercy to the defeated and having compassion for the weak.

Lion Tiger: Referring to a lion and tiger, it symbolizes being merciless to the enemy but compassionate and inclusive toward the weak, echoing the balance between strength and kindness.

Caress, Caress, Military Academy: Represents embracing and loving the Korea Military Academy with pride and dedication, fostering a spirit of affection and continuity of the Hwarangdae spirit. To make this cheer easier to understand, it can be broken down as follows:

ROKA! Veni, Vidi, Vici.

Strong and resilient Korea Military Academy!

With powerful and courageous spirit, we advance with unyielding determination and willpower.

Go forward and create victory, leaving the enemy in ruins.

But let us show mercy to those who surrender, like a lion or a tiger.

My beloved Korea Military Academy! Our Korea Military Academy!

When the athletes were about to depart, everyone would rise to boost their morale with powerful cheers and songs. The cheer songs, along with the Korea Military Academy's anthem, are forever etched in our hearts.

Make way, step aside, our warriors march forward!

The fighting spirit of the KMA shakes the world.

The laurel wreath of victory is ours.

Victory! Victory! Only victory is our pride!

The results of the sports festival of the three military academies were often in favor of the Korea Military Academy, as it had a larger number of cadets. The Korea Military Academy selected 240 cadets annually, while the Naval and Air Force Academies each selected 100, making the number of cadets at the Korea Military Academy more than twice as many.

The sports festival of the 3 Academies at Dongdaemun Stadium

When winning the overall championship, the long procession from Dongdaemun Stadium to the Korea Military Academy at Taereung shook the ground and vibrated with excitement. All vehicles turned on their lights and honked their horns as they marched, with Seoul citizens stepping out to applaud. Winning would grant all cadets a special leave. The discipline between upperclassmen and underclassmen would soften, changing the atmosphere of the school. Along with the sports festival of the three military academies, the brotherly bond among the Army,

Navy, and Air Force cadets was strengthened, and it was believed that if the enemy ever provoked, a highly efficient joint operation would ensure victory and bring success to the nation.

5. Daily Test System

One of the most challenging aspects of cadet life was the daily test system. The Korea Military Academy's academic department was a test hell. Daily tests, final exams, midterms, and end-of-term exams… in every exam, if a cadet scored below 67, which is two-thirds of the total 100 points, they would have to take a retake exam. If they failed the retake exam, they would be expelled.

The daily test is a system where the academic department assigns review and preview tasks, and the tests are conducted daily before class to check the completion of these tasks. If a cadet fails to review or preview the material, they will fail the Daily Test, and if this happens repeatedly, they will have to take a retake exam. Although it was an extremely burdensome system, it created an atmosphere where studying could not be avoided, and cadets took pride in having more fulfilling lessons than most university courses.

If there wasn't enough time for review and preview, cadets studied even after bedtime by applying for extra study hours. At 10:00 PM, all the lights in the dormitory would be turned off, and cadets who had applied for extra study hours would go to a designated place to continue their studies. However, the extra study time was limited to a maximum of two hours. In addition to the Daily Test, there were also midterm and final exams. After each chapter, a test would be given. The academic department made it impossible to endure without studying.

Once, while running, I sprained my ankle. When I went to the hospital, the diagnosis was that I needed a cast and a few days of hospitalization. After being hospitalized for five days, it was difficult to catch up with the coursework. To avoid falling behind other cadets, I had to apply for extra study hours. Since the two-hour limit on study time was not enough, I studied for hours under the faint light that leaked through the bathroom window, which helped me catch up with the coursework.

When General Benfreet established the Korea Military Academy, it was modeled after the United States Military Academy at West Point, so in terms of both facilities and education, it was of the highest level in South Korea. All experimental materials were received as free aid from the United States, and the latest equipment came in, making it more advanced than any domestic university. Completing the entire 4-year curriculum granted a Bachelor of Science degree, so in the field of science, it surpassed Seoul National University's College of Engineering.

Life in the Academic Department
(I am standing second from the right in the second row.)

In the first and second years, the curriculum was primarily focused on liberal arts subjects. In the third year, based on the foundational knowledge learned in the first and second years, subjects such as materials science, fluid mechanics, thermodynamics, atomic physics, solid mechanics, and electrical engineering were taught. In the fourth year, the focus shifted to engineering experiments, including electrical engineering, automotive engineering, civil engineering, and OSC experiments. While also studying theories and critiques of ideologies such as communist thought and Marxism-Leninism, students were able to study subjects that were not covered in general universities.

Subjects and credits required per year

1st Year		2nd Year	
Subjects	Credits	Subjects	Credits
Algebra	3	Differential Equations	1
Spherical Trigonometry	2	Theory of Functions	3
Calculus	4	Advanced Calculus	2
Analytical Geometry	2	Statistics	3
Integral Calculus	4	Physics	8
Differential Equations	3	Physics Lab	1
Natural Science	4	Chemistry	8
Basic Military Science	2	Chemistry Lab	1
Engineering Mechanics	2	Surveying	3
Korean Literature	4	Surveying Practice	1
Cultural History	6	National Defense Geography	3
English	8	Second Foreign Language	4
Military Studies	2	Philosophy	3

Physical Education	3	English	6
		Psychology	2
		Physical Education	2
		Military Studies	2
General Studies	51		53
Cumulative General Studies	51		104
Military Training	6.5		6.5
Discipline	5.2		6
Total	62.7		65.5
Cumulative Total	62.7		128.2

3rd Year		4th Year	
Subjects	Credits	Subjects	Credits
Atomic Physics	6	Electronic Engineering	6
Engineering Mechanics	4	Electronics Lab	1
Mechanics of Materials	3	Weapons Engineering	3.5
Mechanics of Materials Lab	0.5	Industrial Materials Science	1
Thermodynamics	4	Automotive Engineering	1
Thermodynamics Lab	0.5	Structural Design	3
Fluid Mechanics	3	Structural Mechanics	3
Fluid Mechanics Lab	0.5	Reinforced Concrete	1.5
Circuit Theory	3.5	Military Strategy	8
Electrical Machinery	3	Psychology	2

Electrical Engineering Lab	0.5	Elective (1)	2
Economics	4	Critique of Communism	4
English	4	Elective (2)	2
Political Science	4	Military Studies	2
Law	4	Physical Education	1
Psychology	2	Exercise	1
Military Science	2		
Physical Education	1		
General Studies	50.5		46
Cumulative General Studies	154.5		200.5
Military Training	6.5		6.5
Discipline	6		6
Total	63		58.5
Cumulative Total	191.2		249.7

Source: Biographies of the Korea Military Academy 23rd Class, 1997, p.31

The Korea Military Academy started as a military English school after the liberation. It was converted into the National Defense Guard Officer School in May 1946, and in September of the same year, it was renamed the Korea Military Academy. In 1949, it was restructured into a four-year regular program. However, due to the Korean War, the program was not implemented until 1951, when the 11th class of cadets was selected in Jinhae. In June 1954, the academy moved to Taereung, the Hwarangdae. Starting with the 11th class, cadets had to complete the necessary credits for a four-year university degree and were awarded a Bachelor of Science degree, in accordance with the Officer School Establishment Act. Because the Bachelor of Science degree was awarded at the level of a four-year university or higher, the subjects and credits required per year were higher than those at other universities. The cadet life, which involved 24-hour boarding, meant that cadets spent more time studying compared to regular universities.

In the beginning, cadets were taught by inviting professors from regular universities to provide instruction. However, over time, outstanding cadets were sent to domestic and international universities to earn master's and doctoral degrees, and they were then utilized as professors within the academy.

Overseas Education of the 23rd Class of the Korea Military Academy

Name	School	Name	School
Lim Young-hwan	Harvard University, U.S.	Lee Jae	University of Minnesota, U.S.
Jeong Gi-ho	Catholic University, U.S.	Min Seong-gi	Catholic University, U.S.

Song Su-seop	University of Georgia, U.S.	Gwak Yun-geun	University of Texas, U.S.
An Seong-cheong	Catholic University, U.S.	Lee Sang-do	Catholic University, U.S.
Park Seung-il	University of Arizona, U.S.	Na Gi-san	University of Pittsburgh, U.S.
Hong Seong-won	University of Colorado, U.S.	Jo Hyo-nam	University of Michigan, U.S.
Lim Ho-kwon	Catholic University, U.S.	Lee Young-gil	Beijing Foreign Studies University, China
Jeong Jin-won	University of Southern California, U.S.	Yu Je-hyun	University of Michigan, U.S.
On Chang-il	University of Kansas, U.S.	Jeong Ji-yong	Western University, U.S.
Song Young-jun	University of Texas, U.S.	Cha Kimoon	Troy University, U.S.

Source: Biographies of the Korea Military Academy 23rd Class, 1997, p.33

Our classmates who had excellent academic records in the Academic Department were given the opportunity to study at domestic and international universities after graduating from the Korea Military Academy and serving as platoon leaders for one year. After earning master's and doctoral degrees from foreign universities, most of them were assigned as professors in the Academic Department at the Korea Military Academy. There is a prestigious foreign military college course that every soldier would like to attend. It is a course at an advanced country's army college to introduce their military systems. Among them, the most popular course is the U.S. Command and General Staff College, and the classmates who completed this course were Kang Seung-gil, Kim Hak-young, Noh Dong-jun, On Chang-il, Lee Bu-jik, Yu Je-hyun, Jeong Jeong-taek, and Cha Kimoon.

6. The Heart-Throbbing Hwarang Festival

Cadets were required to study hard, but on weekends, they had opportunities for outings and passes, and there were vacations in both the summer and winter. On Saturdays, after conducting barracks inspections and cadet parades, cadets were allowed to go out. During the barracks inspection, senior cadets, wearing white gloves, would run their hands along the window sills, and if any dust was found, the cadet would have to undergo a re-inspection. The rifles also had to be polished until they shone brightly, and only then could a cadet pass the inspection and be allowed to go out. The opportunity for outings served as a motivation, so cadets put all their effort into preparing for the inspections to avoid failing.

Once cadets passed the barracks inspection, they would put

on their formal cadet uniforms and gather on the parade ground. This was to participate in the regular weekly parade. During this time, tourists from outside would come, and cadets' families and significant others would attend the parade. Afterward, visits and outings were allowed.

Cadet Parade

Jeong gwan, The Author, Lee Jae

I had no visitors and no place to go in Seoul for an outing. My alma mater, Daeryun High School, was not co-educational, so I had no opportunities to date. Moreover, being focused solely on my studies, I didn't have the leisure to look around. On weekends, I would always spend my time reading books or exercising in the cadet battalion. Occasionally, when I went out to Seoul, my only enjoyment was visiting movie theaters or art galleries with friends from the same dormitory. When returning after an outing, I had to take a bus from Cheongnyangni. On Sunday evenings, many cadets would be rushing around, trying to catch the right time for their return.

A cadet must strictly adhere to the "three prohibitions." These prohibitions are alcohol, cigarettes, and women. Cadets are not allowed to drink, smoke, or get married. During the summer vacation of the third year, I broke the three prohibitions and drank alcohol for the first time. I used my vacation to travel to Jeju Island with Cadet Kim Moon-gi. We took a C-54 transport plane from Yeouido Airfield to Jeju Island. At that time, Yeouido was a military airfield. Since we were poor cadets, we decided to use the military transport plane.

After landing at Jeju Airport, we followed the 5.16 Road and explored Seogwipo, Hallasan Mountain, and the entire island of Jeju for the first time in my life. After hiking up Hallasan, I still get a little dizzy when I think about getting lost on the way down. Being in an unfamiliar place like Jeju made me feel a bit more relaxed, so for the first time, I broke the three prohibitions and stopped by a draft beer house to have a glass of beer.

As graduation approached in my fourth year, a festival called the 'Hwarang Festival' was held. For this festival, cadets were required to participate with a female partner. This put cadets without girlfriends in a dilemma. I, too, was one of those cadets without a girlfriend, and I found myself troubled. I was envious of the cadets whose girlfriends or partners would visit and go on outings with them. As the Hwarang Festival drew nearer, it became a situation where everyone had to bring someone along.

At that time, I asked the younger sister of my senior, Cha Ki-jun, from the 21st class, who was attending Seoul Women's University of Education (now renamed Sejong University). Cha Ki-jun, whose hometown was Ulsan, wasn't closely related to me, but during vacations, he would often visit Ulsan to spend time with his family. His parents, who ran a large rice mill, treated me like a son, so I had a comfortable relationship with them.

Through the introduction of his sister, I found a partner for the Hwarang Festival named Yoon Suk-young, a student at Seoul Women's University of Education. She was the only daughter of a bank president from Daejeon, and she was a petite, traditional-looking woman who looked great in a hanbok. Her delicate figure and oval-shaped face reminded me of her mother. She wasn't very talkative, but when she made a joke, she would cover her mouth with a smile, which made her very likable to everyone. She had a reserved, yet charming Korean-style femininity, and anyone who met her for the first time would want to get to know her. When she attended the Hwarang Festival dressed in hanbok, she stood out so much that she became the center of attention among my classmates.

Hwarang Festival

After the Hwarang Festival, weekends became something to look forward to, as I now had someone to spend time with during outings. She was from Daejeon and was living on her own in Hwakyang-dong near Seoul Women's University of Education. Along with my fellow cadet In Seong-gyeong, who was in the same situation as me, we visited her dormitory and were treated to a homemade lunch. With a girlfriend just before graduation, every day became filled with joy and happiness.

However, after graduating from the Korea Military Academy and being assigned to the front, communication between us ceased. After becoming a platoon leader at the front, I immediately found myself in the midst of the January 21st Blue House raid crisis, leading to an ongoing series of busy days. Then, the armed infiltration incidents in Uljin and Samcheok occurred, and I spent most of my time deep in the mountains of Seoraksan. Later, I was sent to Vietnam war, and when I returned two years later, she had already become a middle school teacher and had gotten married. The Hwarang Festival remains an unforgettable event that leaves cadets with romance and lasting memories. It was a grand festival at Hwarangdae, where cadets, bound by the strict "three prohibitions." rules, could invite their lovers and girlfriends, spend time together, and even form new connections. It was a heart-throbbing festival for all cadets.

7. The Star of Hwarangdae

After the Hwarang Festival ended and graduation approached, the fourth-year cadets were invited to the Blue House. President Park Chung-hee and First Lady Yuk Young-soo personally hosted a graduation celebration party at the Nokjiwon garden of the Blue House. Cadets from all three military academies were invited, making it a joyful reunion after a long time. President Park and the First Lady shook hands with each of us and came to each table to share warm conversations. As a former military academy graduate and soldier himself, the president had a special affection and interest in the cadets.

Blue House Party　　　　　　　　The Star of Hwarangdae

On February 23, 1967, the graduation ceremony was held at the Hwarang Parade Ground amidst great public interest and blessings. With President Park Chung-hee and the First Lady in attendance, the Bachelor of Science degrees were conferred, and the commissioning ceremony for second lieutenants took place simultaneously. It was still cold in February, yet the cadets stood at attention without the slightest movement throughout the outdoor ceremony. I vividly remembered attending the graduation of the 19th military academy class in basic training uniform, when the young freshman cadets fainted and were carried out on stretchers—and now, four full years later, it was our turn to graduate. Following the graduation ceremony, the Star of the Hwarangdae event created yet another festive atmosphere. It was a farewell celebration in which the juniors bid farewell to their seniors by forming a large star-shaped formation. As they listened to the farewell songs sung by their juniors, the seniors tossed their well-worn cadet caps—used throughout the past four years—high into the sky and replaced them with new officer caps. The Star of Hwarangdae ceremony reached its emotional climax with a tribute at the statue of Kang Jae-gu. Major Kang Jae-gu is a living hero in the hearts of the cadets, having sacrificed his life to shield his men from a grenade during pre-deployment training for the Vietnam War. A graduate of the 16th class of the Korea Military Academy, he was serving as the commander of the 10th Company, 1st Regiment of the Capital Division's (Tiger Division) on October 4, 1965, just before deployment. During a grenade-throwing exercise, a grenade thrown by Private Park Hae-cheon soared too high and fell toward the gathered company members. Most of the troops were within the effective blast radius, and heavy casualties were expected. The terrain made it impossible to catch the grenade by hand or kick it away. At that critical moment, Kang Jae-gu threw himself onto the grenade, covering it with his own body, and was instantly killed in the explosion.[1]

Major Kang Jae-gu Memorial / A film

While he was alive, he came to the Korea Military Academy and gave a lecture to us, his juniors, saying, "A soldier should live a short but intense life." As an exemplary officer, he came to Hwarangdae while serving as a company commander and gave

---

1 Global World Encyclopedia, Beomhan Publishing, 2004, p.13.

us mental training.

At my graduation ceremony from the Korea Military Academy, my father, mother, sister Cha Jeong-sook, and her friends attended to celebrate. They had come up to Seoul from my hometown a few days earlier just to attend the ceremony. While staying at an inn, they took the opportunity to do some sightseeing in Seoul and visited the academy for the first time.

My family and relatives at the graduation ceremony

After the graduation ceremony, Major Kim Yeon-geun, a professor in the Department of History at the academy, invited us to his home. Major Kim Yeon-geun was my senior from Daeryun School, had graduated as part of the 11th class of the military academy, majored in history at Seoul National

University, earned a doctoral degree, and was now teaching history to cadets. When I was in my second year at the academy, he found out that I was his junior from Daeryun and called me in to offer encouragement, which became the beginning of our connection. After that, his wife, knowing I had no family in Seoul, warmly cooked meals for me and showed me kindness and affection.

Saying that we should express our gratitude to people like them, my mother took dried persimmons she had brought and went to see Major Kim Yeon-geun. Even afterward, she would always ask after him, saying she could never forget the warm hospitality she had received at that time.

It was difficult to get into the Korea Military Academy, but graduating was even harder. Cadets were expelled for violating the honor code or the three-prohibition system, or for failing to keep up with academic performance. Although 244 cadets were admitted at the beginning, only 177 graduated.

Part II

Guardians of the Nation

Chapter 1

•

| The Years as a Company Officer |

1. Officer Basic Course at the Infantry School

Upon graduating from the Korea Military Academy, cadets were commissioned as second lieutenants and headed to their assigned branch schools. The branches were initially classified into five combat arms. To receive training in the Officer Basic Course (OBC) suited to their respective specialties, officers were sent to various locations such as Gwangju, Daejeon, and Gimhae. As an infantry officer, I went to the Infantry School in Gwangju.

Initial Branch Assignment for the 23rd Class

Branches	Infantry	Artillery	Armor	Engineer	Signal
Number of people	92	42	3	25	15

Source: Biographies of the Korea Military Academy 23rd Class, 1997, p.25

The Infantry School, located at Sangmudae in Gwangju, was widely known as the cradle of the combat arms, as it was situated alongside the Artillery and Armor Schools. Since unmarried junior officers received training there, it was common for them to naturally form relationships with young women from Gwangju. Many officer families had ties to Gwangju precisely because the branch schools for junior officers were located there.

One unforgettable part of the Infantry Officer Basic Course was the guerrilla training conducted at the Dongbuk Training Center in the Gurye and Gokseong regions. This grueling training, like going through hell, included escape and evasion, survival skills, and more. After being starved for several days, we had to navigate toward our objectives day and night under harsh conditions. Since enemies were ambushed along the easier routes, we had to traverse rugged mountainous terrain, catching and eating snakes and frogs along the way. After enduring such a demanding course, we gained the confidence to overcome any situation we might face in the field.

The final phase of the Officer Basic Course was the comprehensive field training exercise. It was a culmination of the individual combat, squad-level, and platoon-level tactics we had learned. After spending several days living in personal tents during this exercise, we were returning to base by vehicle when an accident occurred involving the truck ahead of us on a curved road. A second 2.5 ton truck, packed with second lieutenants, had overturned 180 degrees into a barley field on the side of the road. The truck's wheels were spinning in the air, and all the second lieutenants onboard had been thrown under the open-top vehicle. The barley field was completely drenched in blood. The injured were transported to Gwangju Military Hospital, but many were unconscious. Although they later regained consciousness, their mental state was far from normal. General Jeong Rae-hyuk, the commander of the Combat Arms Training Command, visited the hospital and questioned the patients.

"What do you want to eat the most?"

"I want to eat monkey brains."

"Do you know who your commander is?"

"Why are you asking when you're the danm commander?"

General Jeong Rae-hyuk was the commandant of the Korea Military Academy when we were cadets, but the patients didn't recognize him and gave irrelevant answers. The entire Army showed concern for the wounded, and every effort was made to restore their mental state. The most authoritative military doctors from across the army gathered to take the utmost care of the patients, and as a result, all of them recovered to the point where they could resume normal military service. Not a single person was left behind, and all were reassigned to the front lines. The classmates who were injured at that time later performed even better in their duties.

Infantry school OBC training (left: Lee Jong-gyu, right: The Author)

After completing the Officer Basic Course, we were given a few days of leave before being assigned to frontline units. During this leave, I traveled around the country's famous mountains and landmarks with Second Lieutenant Lee Jong-gyu. There were two classmates named Lee Jong-gyu, so we referred to them as "Big Lee Jong-gyu" and "Small Lee Jong-gyu" based on their height. The one who traveled with me was Small Lee Jong-gyu.

One night during our trip, we stayed at a hermitage of the Jikjisa Temple in Gimcheon, which remains a vivid memory. In the foothills, white storks perched on the pine trees, turning the entire landscape white. The sound of the wind in the valley at dawn felt like entering a paradise. We spent the night at Second Lieutenant Lee Jong-gyu's house in Hadong, then continued our journey through Jinju and along the southern coast. Lee Jong-gyu's mother treated me like her own son, showing me great kindness and care. When we arrived at Haeinsa Temple in Hapcheon, we stayed at my home. My father, mother, and the entire family warmly welcomed us. After the leave, he was assigned to the 11th Division, while I was assigned to the 2nd Division. All officers from the Korea Military Academy were assigned to frontline divisions as platoon leaders.

2. Three Musketeers to the 17th Regiment

The newly commissioned second lieutenants heading to the frontline were assigned as platoon leaders, commanding actual troops for the first time. Although the unit commanders clamored for more officers from the Korea Military Academy, the number was limited, so they were evenly distributed among the units. Three officers were assigned to each regiment, with one officer assigned to each battalion. I, along with Second Lieutenants Kim Myung-sae and Kim Moon-so, was assigned to the 17th Regiment of the 2nd Division located in Inje. Second Lieutenant Kim Myung-sae, a graduate of Jeonju High School, was an exemplary officer who set a model for others during his time as a cadet at the Korea Military Academy. Even after commissioning, he continued to earn respect from his classmates for his thoughtful and considerate character. Second Lieutenant Kim Moon-so, a graduate of Seoul High School with excellent academic achievements, was a Rugby player during his time at the Korea Military Academy. Although we didn't have much time together as cadets, he became one of my closest classmates after our commissioning. He had a great sense of humor, and the more we got to know each other, the more we appreciated his warm, down-to-earth personality. The three of us platoon leaders were affectionately called the "Three Musketeers" by the 17th Regiment.

When we, the newly commissioned second lieutenants, arrived at the division headquarters of the 2nd Division in Yanggu, everything felt unfamiliar. We stood around, looking confused, as we observed the soldiers passing by. While waiting to go to our regiment, all the other officers heading to different units had left, and only the three of us, heading to the 17th Regiment, remained. After a while, a major arrived in a jeep and, with a gruff voice, called out, "Hey! You lieutenants, get over here and get in!" We saluted and climbed into the jeep. During the ride, the major said nothing, sitting in the back seat, silently observing our behavior. Since this was our first encounter with a superior officer, none of us dared to speak, and an uneasy silence filled the vehicle. Later, we learned that the major was the personnel officer of the 17th Regiment.

After about an hour of driving from the division toward Inje, it was already late in the evening. The personnel officer dropped the three of us off in Inje city and told us to report to the regiment the next morning. Stranded in the unfamiliar town of Inje, we had no idea where to go. First, we found a place to sleep at a guesthouse, and then we surveyed the town. We were curious to see what Inje, the place where we would begin our first assignment, looked like.

It was during the time when the saying, "When will I ever get out of Inje, I can't stand it," was popular. Inje and the nearby area called Wontong were located north of the 38th parallel, and soldiers often said that once they were assigned there, it was difficult to leave until their discharge. As a result, it was a frontline area that everyone dreaded serving in.

After taking a walk around Inje, we entered a bar that, during our time as cadets, we had never been able to visit due to the restrictions of the 3 prohibitions system. It was a shabby place with a strong rural smell. Young women, with thick makeup, greeted us warmly, saying, "Welcome!" The three of us, thinking we should properly report to our first unit, followed the rhythm of the traditional music the women were playing and, using chopsticks, tapped on the table while drinking Makgeolli. True to the lesson we had been taught, "No matter how drunk you get, you must tie your boots properly," we made sure to enter the 17th Regiment headquarters the next morning at the scheduled time.

The regimental personnel officer had us report to Colonel Jeong Heon-guk (Korea Military Academy 10th class), the regimental commander. Through his briefing, the regimental commander emphasized, "Our Infantry 17th Regiment has a proud history and tradition, having participated in the Incheon Landing Operation during the Korean War and being the first to retake Seoul," urging us to serve with pride. After completing the report to the compassionate and thoughtful Colonel Jeong Heon-guk, who left a lasting impression on us, the junior officers, we were assigned to our respective battalions. Lieutenant Kim Moon-so was assigned to the 1st Battalion, 1st Company, I was assigned to the 2nd Battalion, 7th Company, and Lieutenant Kim Myung-sae was assigned to the 3rd Battalion, 9th Company.

17th Infantry Regiment at the Incheon Landing Operation

The 7th Company I was assigned to had no electricity, so kerosene lamps were used to light the barracks. After sleeping at night, my nostrils would be blackened from the soot of the kerosene lamps. Since there was no separate office for the platoon leader, one corner of the barracks was partitioned with wooden planks. Heating was done by lighting a fire in the pechika stove with coal dust. To prepare kindling for the fire, after training, all the soldiers would carry armfuls of wood back to the unit.

When the three of us were assigned to the regiment, the atmosphere in the unit became lively. As the newly commissioned platoon leaders assigned to each battalion carried out principled unit management, other platoon leaders followed suit, and this changed the overall atmosphere of the regiment. Most importantly, since the rice and rations served in the mess hall were no longer leaked outside, the soldiers received proper portions and were all pleased. Before we arrived, the officers had taken the main and side dishes, so even if beef soup was served, it became "beef soup with no beef," with no meat to be found. The soldiers always complained that they were hungry because there was never enough rice, but after the three of us arrived and took shifts as duty officers, we strictly supervised the mess hall, ensuring that no rice or rations were leaked outside, and the unit became one where proper distribution was maintained.

My Battalion Commander was Lieutenant Colonel Choi Yeon-sik, who was from the 11th class of the Korea Military Academy. Lieutenant Colonel Choi took good care of me, offering me a room in the battalion commander's quarters and treating me like a younger brother. The battalion commander's wife also showed kindness by having the duty soldier warm up my room and even bringing me a silk blanket.

My 7th Company was ordered to guard the Third Army Corps Headquarters, located in Gwandae-ri. At that time, it was a period when armed spies frequently appeared, so the security of the headquarters was rotated between subordinate units. Next to the army corps headquarters, the U.S. Military Advisory Group (KMAG) was stationed, and our platoon was also tasked with guarding their compound. The KMAG commander called me over, thanked me for providing security for their unit, and invited me to have a meal at the U.S. officers' mess. From that point on, I had the opportunity to understand the lifestyle and culture of the U.S. military while dining with them.

Once, an accident occurred at the army corps headquarters' guard post, where the stove overheated and completely burned down the building. The stove's sprayer malfunctioned, causing oil to leak all at once, and a newly assigned soldier, in his panic, mishandled the aftermath, which led to a large fire. As the platoon leader, I took responsibility for the incident and was summoned by the Criminal Investigation Department (CID) of the army corps for an investigation. After the inquiry, I found myself in a situation where I was about to be sent to prison. I resigned myself, thinking my military career was over, but then

I was told that the CID commander wanted to see me. When I entered the CID commander's office, a stern Major sat there, looking me up and down, and asked me several questions.

"Are you Officer Cha Kimoon from the 23rd class of the Military Academy?"

"Yes! That's correct."

"Why did you burn down the guard post?"

"The stove sprayer malfunctioned, and the oil leaked. The new recruit mishandled the situation, leading to the accident. However, I take full responsibility as the platoon leader. I apologize."

He asked me in detail about my personal background, then threw the investigation report into the fire and told me to go back and do my duties properly. He even invited me to his quarters for dinner over the weekend. Later, I found out that the Criminal Investigation Officer was Major Ahn Jong-ha, a graduate of the 12th class of the Military Academy. Just when I thought I was going straight to prison and my military career was over, Major Ahn made everything disappear as if nothing had happened. I was so grateful when he even invited me for dinner that I almost cried.

When I went to the Criminal Investigation Officer's quarters over the weekend, his wife had prepared a nice dinner and greeted me along with her beautiful younger sister. The young woman, who resembled the beautiful wife, shyly glanced at me while observing her brother-in-law's reactions, sending me a friendly look. Major Ahn Jong-ha had arranged the dinner to introduce me to his sister-in-law.

However, our company was soon ordered to move to Mountain Seorak to carry out an anti-guerrilla operation. With a heavy heart, I had no choice but to head to Mountain Seorak. Even at night, as I lay down to sleep, the image of the beautiful young woman lingered in my mind. Due to the operation in the Misiryeong and Sinheungsa areas, I could not leave the mountains until my term as platoon leader was over, and after that, I never saw the criminal investigation officer's sister-in-law again. During this period, armed infiltrators from North Korea were causing turmoil.

The most significant event was the January 21st Blue House raid. On January 21, 1968, 31 armed North Korean commandos from the 124th Army Special Forces attempted to assassinate President Park Chung-hee by raiding the Blue House. They were armed with grenades and submachine guns and infiltrated into the capital area, crossing the demilitarized zone while dressed in South Korean military uniforms. They were stopped by police on duty during a routine check as they attempted to pass through the Jahamun gate near the Seogumjeong pass. When their true identities were revealed, they threw grenades at the police and indiscriminately fired submachine guns. They also threw grenades at a city bus passing by, killing many citizens on their way home.

The military immediately declared a state of emergency and deployed to the scene, where they killed 29 infiltrators, captured one, and one managed to escape to the North. As a result of the incident, many civilians were injured or killed. That night, Police Chief Choi Gyu-sik, who was overseeing emergency duty at the scene, was killed by enemy gunfire.[1] The only infiltrator captured that day, Kim Shin-jo, realized he had been deceived by Kim Il-sung's false propaganda and subsequently defected, eventually becoming a pastor. Park Jae-kyung, who escaped to the North, was reportedly treated as a hero in North Korea, eventually rising to the rank of major general and becoming the deputy minister of the Ministry of People's Armed Forces.

On October 30, 1968, 120 armed North Korean commandos infiltrated the Uljin and Samcheok areas. Many innocent

---

[1] Son Jeong-mok, "The January 21 Incident and Its Impact," Urban Issues, Vol. 37, Issue 409, p. 94.

civilians were killed by them. In a remote house at the foot of Mt. Gyeibang in Na Dong-ri, Yongpyeong-myeon, Pyeongchang-gun, Gangwon-do, 7 to 8 armed commandos broke into the home of Lee Seok-woo (37 years old). Lee's wife, Joo Dae-ha (34 years old), their second son Seung-bok (9 years old), third son Seung-su (7 years old), and eldest daughter Seung-ja (4 years old) were all brutally murdered.[2]

Infiltration by armed North Korean commandos
in Uljin and Samcheok
(Chosun Ilbo, December 11, 1968)

---

2   Chosun Ilbo, December 11, 1968.

At that time, I was carrying out an operation to block armed North Korean infiltrators fleeing north along the Baekdu Mountain Range around Misiryeong and Sinheungsa. In the freezing winter, we dug trenches and hastily built ondol heating systems. Ondol was the best method for ensuring warmth in such conditions. Heavy snowfall had cut off supply routes. The platoon members had to learn how to survive locally as supplies were scarce. We endured hunger by digging up wild yam roots from the snow and eating the red mountain berries that remained buried in the snow, waiting for supplies to arrive.

My messenger, after going on a mission, would cook rice in a mess kit and bring it back, keeping it close to his chest to keep it warm, offering it to me so I could have a hot meal. However, as the platoon leader, I couldn't eat alone. Even though I was starving, I couldn't eat the rice he had carefully prepared by myself. I decided to share it with my platoon members, one spoonful at a time, and we promised to do our best to catch the enemy together. We inspected every vehicle passing over Misiryeong. This was to ensure that no enemy vehicles passed by, as they might hijack them. At night, we found many illegal vehicles transporting logs to Seoul or charcoal made from oak trees. They left boxes of squid and hairtail fish, claiming to be providing them as a morale-boosting gift, saying they knew the soldiers conducting counter infiltration operations were having a hard time. However, I refused all these fish boxes, which were not pure gifts but bribes.

In the midst of carrying out these operations, I was able to capture all the armed infiltrators who were heading north through the snow. In winter, operations were extremely advantageous for us. Following the footprints in the snow, we were certain to find armed infiltrators hiding under rocks. By using tactics like "rabbit hunting" and snaring, we surrounded them, and the infiltrators, who had been starving for days, were completely wiped out.

Counter infiltration operation

After our platoon successfully completed the counter infiltration operation, we returned to our garrison in Inje. Upon finishing a year as a platoon leader, I was given the opportunity to transfer to a different branch. Some of my classmates transferred to branches such as the military police, finance, or legal. I was also encouraged by close acquaintances to transfer to the military police. However, I was determined to continue advancing in the combat arms in order to pursue my lofty dreams, so I remained in the infantry—the most combat-oriented of all combat branches.

Branch Transfer of the 23rd Class of the Korea Military Academy

Adjutant	1	Kim Jeong-ho
Military Police	2	Lee Jae-hwan, Park Ho-gil
Judge Advocate	1	Lee Sang-do
Information and Education	3	Shim Gi-seop, Park Young-taek, Lee Young-gil
Finance	2	Kim Woo-yeol, Yoon Yong-seop
Anti-Communist Affairs	1	Kim Dong-yoon
KMA Faculty	16	Lim Young-hwan, Lee Jae, On Chang-il, Jeong Gi-ho, Ahn Seong-cheong, Na Gi-san, Hong Seong-won, Kwak Yoon-geun, Cho Hyo-nam, Song Young-jun, Lee Sang-do, Jeong Ji-yong, Kim Moon-so, Min Seong-gi, Song Soo-seop, Shin Hyeong-gang

Intelligence	9	Kim Moon-gi, Seo Se-ho, Shin Hyun-soo, Park Seung-il, Woo Jong-il, Park Bang-woong, Shin Woon-cheol, Noh Si-deok, Choi Jae-rim
National Intelligence Service	6	Kim Seon-tae, Heo Jin-young, Lee Geum-saeng, Kim Sang-deok, Cho Young-shin, Jang Geun-sik

Source: Biographies of the Korea Military Academy 23rd Class, 1997, p.8

3. Vietnamese Language Training School

After completing my duties as a platoon leader in the 17th Regiment of the 2nd Infantry Division, I was assigned as the regiment's operations and training officer. While a platoon leader can lead a unit through physical presence and command, a staff officer must demonstrate creative planning abilities through intellect. Upon receiving the operations and training assignment, I realized I didn't even know how to draft a basic operations message. I steadily learned the job under the guidance of the operations officer. I gave my utmost to every task assigned to me, even staying up through the night if necessary. As I quickly grasped the duties, the regimental commander and staff began to recognize me as a capable officer. While I was carrying out my duties in the operations section, an official notice was issued seeking applicants for airborne training. At the time, I had not been able to complete airborne training during my cadet years at the military academy. As a soldier, I had a strong desire to experience airborne training at least once—to parachute down from the sky. I submitted my application right away and went to the First Army Command in Wonju to take the physical fitness test, with the plan to enter the Special Warfare Command's Airborne Training School. However, before I could proceed, an order came from Army Headquarters assigning me to Vietnam war.

The Vietnam War was at a peak, and there was a high demand for junior officers in combat. People believed that once junior officers were sent to Vietnam war, they would all die. In fact, many casualties were being flown back to Korea. A common saying at the time was, "If you go by ship, make sure you come back by ship—don't come back by plane." This saying arose because most troops were transported to Vietnam by ship, while only the dead or wounded returned by plane. Under these circumstances, officers who had graduated from the Korea Military Academy were given deployment orders to Vietnam war unilaterally by Army Headquarters, regardless of their personal wishes. Since it was considered natural for soldiers to go to war, we willingly accepted this system. Out of 177 classmates who graduated as part of the 23rd class of the Korea Military

Academy, excluding those assigned as instructors at the academy, 144 participated in the Vietnam War.

When I went to Army Headquarters to prepare for deployment to Vietnam, the personnel operations officer instructed me to enroll in the Vietnamese Language Training School located in Dongbinggo, Seoul. In Dongbinggo, there was a language education center within the Intelligence School, where Vietnamese was being taught. At the Vietnamese Language Training Center, native Vietnamese speakers served as instructors and taught the language.

The 23rd class of the Korea Military Academy deployed to Vietnam

Year	Number of people	Names
1967	8	Im Yeong-hwan, Kim Gil-sam, Lee Yeong-sik, Jang Pan-yong, Park Bang-ung, Kim Yong-gyeong, Jeong Byeong-tae, Kim Gwon-hu
1968	84	Cha Kimoon, Lee Jeong-gyun, Jang Gil-nam, Lee Yeong-eon, Nam Gi-heon, Shin Hyeon-su, Son Su-tae, Jeong Jeong-taek, Park Yeong-il, Kim Myeong-se, Jeong Hwae-on, Lee Jong-wan, Kwon Yeong-hyo, Kang Jong-pil, In Seong-gyeong, Moon Il-seob, Moon Dong-myeong, Son Mun-seong, Kim Seok-jae, Park Yeong-ik, Ahn Seong-yong, Jeong Yeong-jin, Noh Bu-ryeong, Lee Nam-sin, Jeong Gi-ho, Bae Ui-wung, Seol Yeong-gil, Park Ju-yeong, Park Seung-il, Noh Nam-seob, Jo Tae-hyeong, Kim Gang-hwang, Park Chang-su, Kwon Dae-po, Yang Yeong-bu, Yang Yeong-gi, Lee Jong-seon, Lee Bu-jik, Gu Il-cheol, Kim Jeong-won, Kim Yong-gu, Park No-cheol, Jeon Sang-yeol, Shim Gi-seop, Park No-yang, Han Jeong-ju, Jang

		Dong-uk, Yang Gil-yong, Choi Jae-rim, Kang Seung-gil, Jeong Wan-chae, Cha Yeong-seop, Jeong Myeong-hwa, Choi Gi-chang, Yang Sang-jin, Kim Dong-mun, Lee Geum-saeng, Park Seong-il, Kim Yeong-won, Jeong Bok-seop, Kim Sang-deok, Park Jeong-seok, Jo Yeong-sin, Lee Geon-bu, Kim Seong-yu, Jo Ui-wung, Park Hye-cheol, Kim Yo-ung, Ban Won-joong, Ha Jeong-gon, Park Seung-bu, Shin Un-cheol, Song O-seob, Lee Seong-woo, Choi Su-mok, Jeong Jin-won, Jo Yeong-hwi, Yoo Je-hyeon, Jeong Ji-yong, Song Yeong-jun, Kim Jae-ik, Park Hee-bok, Lee Jong-gyu (Big), Lee Jong-gyu (Small)
1969	26	Kim Hak-yeong, Lee Yeong-il, Moon Jong-yun, Kim Mun-ki, Gil Yeong-cheol, Lee Won-rak, Kim Dong-yun, Song Su-seob, Kim Tae-un, Lee Seong-hui, Gu Ja-yeol, Yoo Han-ju, Joo Seon-man, Kim Gu-woong, Choi Yeong-bu, Kim Eung-gyeom, Oh Ju-ui, Kim Yeong-ri, Ije Won, Kwon Jeong-haeng, Park Jong-gyu, Kwon Cheol-ho, Han Gwang-so, Lee Yeong-gil, Yang Chang-yeol, Choi Gi-ok
1970	10	Oh Yeong-gwan, Kim Hyeon-su, Noh Dong-jun, Heo Yeol, Kim Jung-seo, Moon Chang-hoon, Jang U-gyun, Park Ho-gil, Kim Ho-kwon, Kim Seong-yong
1971	6	Jeon Gwan, Kim Dae-hoon, Yoo Seung-woo, Park Jeong-cheol, Park Hyeong-gyu, Lee Jae-hwan
1972	10	Hong Jeong-heon, Jeong Jeong-taek, Kim Woo-yeol, Lee Mun-won, Jang Gwang-nam, Woo Yeong-mu, Kim Yeong-geol, Lee Chun-woong, Jeong Jeong-sang, Noh Si-deok
Sum	144	

Source: Biographies of the Korea Military Academy 23rd Class, 1997, p.23

Among them, there was a teacher named Jo Ok-sook, born between a Vietnamese woman and a Korean man. Jo Ok-sook was born and raised in Vietnam and was educated there, and she was a beautiful woman, which made her very popular among the students. Her aunt lived in Seoul, and her younger brother,

Jo Man-yong, also came to Seoul to study at his aunt's house, following his older sister. Since my Vietnamese language skills were superior to those of the other students, I was able to spend a lot of time with them during holidays. On weekends, I had the opportunity to take the still unmarried Jo Ok-sook and her younger brother, Jo Man-yong, to visit folk villages and palaces, teaching them about Korean culture and history. I was also able to practice conversational Vietnamese while traveling around the city of Seoul.

I lived in a boarding house near the terminal of bus number 42 in Bogwang-dong, right next to the language training center at the Intelligence School. The boarding house was within walking distance of the training school. One time, while walking to the school with my backpack on and memorizing Vietnamese words, a military jeep suddenly screeched to a stop in front of me. On the jeep's front bumper, I could clearly see the markings "5160 Unit No. 1." Inside the vehicle was a colonel wearing dark sunglasses.

"Where is that officer going?"

"Yes! I'm heading to the Vietnamese language education center at the Intelligence School."

"Then get in!"

"What's your name?"

"I'm Second Lieutenant Cha Kimoon."

"Where are you from?"

"I'm from Hapcheon Kyungsangmando."

The colonel dropped me off in front of the gate of the Vietnamese language education center and told me to come visit his house if I had no plans over the weekend, giving me his address. Later, I found out that the 5160 unit was the 30th brigade of the Capital Security Command (later Capital Defense Command), and the person in the jeep was Colonel Chun Doo-hwan, who became the President of the Fifth Republic of Korea. Colonel Chun's house was near my boarding house in Bo-gwang-dong. On weekends, I would sometimes visit and have meals there. After I left for Vietnam, it became harder to approach Colonel Chun. Over time, the distance between a second lieutenant and a colonel, and I no longer had opportunities to get close to him. Moreover, as someone who was not part of Hanahoe, it became impossible for me to cross the high social barriers to reach him.

While receiving Vietnamese language education in Korea and serving in Vietnam war, I was given the opportunity to take an advanced Vietnamese language course at the Vietnamese military language school. The level of Vietnamese I learned was quite advanced, but over time, I forgot it all because I didn't use it.

Vietnamese Language Course (I am standing fifth from the left in the back row).

I graduated at the top of my class from the Korean Army Intelligence School's Vietnamese language education center and then went to Omri, Chuncheon, for deployment to Vietnam war. Omri was where soldiers selected from all units for the Vietnam deployment gathered. It was a place where basic education on Vietnamese culture and local circumstances was provided for soldiers heading to the battlefield for the first time.

4. To the Vietnam war

Upon arriving at Oom-ri in Chuncheon, I was assigned as the platoon leader of the Civil Affairs and Psychological Operations Command by the Ministry of National Defense, under order No. 836 issued on December 9, 1968. Since I had studied Vietnamese, I was assigned to the Civil Affairs and Psychological Operations unit, which played a significant role in the Vietnam War. After completing the necessary procedures, I left Oom-ri training camp, took a train from Chuncheon to Busan. At Busan Port, families lined up in rows to see off the soldiers being sent to Vietnam war. Amid the military band's performance, the military song of the departing units echoed loudly, and the air was filled with a banner reading, "Wishing the Best of Luck to the Soldiers Going to Vietnam war."

> For the defense of the fatherland
> For the reunification of the nation
> Chosen in the name of the country
> Brave soldiers of the Mighty Tiger Division
> Though the sky over Vietnam may be far
> With unwavering patriotism

> We will follow in your footsteps
>
> For the reunification of the nation
>
> The strength we've nurtured
>
> In the name of the country
>
> There is no place we cannot go
>
> Brave soldiers of the Mighty Tiger Division
>
> Under the sky of Vietnam
>
> Divided into the lands of the North and South
>
> Let us show the noble spirit of the Hwarang Corps

This was a military song aimed at boosting the morale of the troops of the Tiger Division (the capital division) and White Horse Division (the 9th Division), who were being replaced. It was the first time in the history of Korea that a military force of more than two combat divisions was sent overseas. The Tiger Division was the first to be deployed, followed by the White Horse Division. As soon as the Tiger Division's military song ended, White Horse Division's song cut through the blue waves.

> Do you know that name, the invincible man
>
> The glorious warriors of White Horse
>
> That earned a brilliant victory

> Raising the banner of justice, high and proud
> Where White Horse goes, there is justice
> The White Horse rides on to the land of Vietnam
> Victory and return, the warriors of Korea
> Do you know that name, the man of reversal
> The glorious warriors of White Horse
> Whose name shines bright
> Raising the banner of freedom, high and proud
> Where White Horse goes, there is freedom
> The White Horse rides on to the land of Vietnam
> Victory and return, the warriors of Korea

On the pier, lovers, reluctant to part, embrace each other, unwilling to let go. A child, carried on her mother's back, waves goodbye to her father with her small, delicate hands. A mother prays with both hands folded, asking for her son's safe return. I, with no one to greet me, quietly watch this scene of parting, when, in the distance, I see someone waving and running toward me. The person who came closer was my high school classmate, Second Lieutenant Jeong Il-woong. He had been commissioned as the ROTC Class 5 and was serving as a translator with the U.S. Military Advisory Group in Busan. He had seen my name on the list of soldiers sent overseas and came running to find me. How much comfort it was to have Jeong Il-woong, my dear friend, by my side during my loneliness. Jeong Il-woong later retired as a high school principal after serving in education, becoming a friend I will never forget.

Tiger Division farewell ceremony   White Horse Division farewell ceremony

The transport ship heading to Vietnam was an enormous vessel. It was the first time I had ever boarded such a large ship. During the 5 night, 6 day journey across the South China Sea towards Vietnam, many soldiers suffered from seasickness. The officers were assigned to the officer quarters, which were like a hotel located in the central part of the ship, but there was no one who wasn't affected by seasickness. I was able to understand how difficult it must be for the naval personnel who always have to be on ships. The meals on board were excellent. The tropical fruits, which I tasted for the first time, helped stimulate our appetite, which had been diminished. The staff working in the dining area were mostly Filipinos, who were very kind and provided excellent service.

On the fifth day after departing from Busan Port, it became almost unbearable. It felt like a marathon runner collapsing at the finish line. If we had to sail for one more day, I felt like I would want to give up everything. All I could think about was getting on land as quickly as possible. On the sixth morning, the green mountains slowly appeared on the horizon, shimmering in the morning sunlight. We were approaching the Vietnamese port of Nha Trang, where we would disembark. The sight of the green forests and land was so welcoming, and the feeling was indescribable.

When I disembarked from the ship, a vehicle from the local unit was waiting for us. Since there were Viet Cong ambushes in various areas, we traveled along an unpaved road under the protection of armed forces, heading towards the Civil-Military Psychological Warfare Unit.

The Vietnam War was not a conventional war but an unconventional one, so most operations involved psychological warfare. The Civil-Military Psychological Warfare Unit used loudspeakers to encourage defection in the mountain regions and dropped leaflets in areas where the Viet Cong were hiding. After conducting a flamethrower operation on the Viet Cong hiding in caves, we used portable loudspeakers to persuade them to come out.

Civil Affairs and Psychological Operations HQ personnel
(I am standing first on the right.)

There were numerous times when we directly fought with Viet Cong who refused to defect and tried to escape in the jungle. Artillery and mortar fire from the allied forces behind us exploded overhead, with the sound of bullets and shells passing above us, as if they might stop my heart. The sound of AK-47 rifle shots fired by the Viet Cong towards us felt as if a bullet was about to lodge into my forehead.

The Viet Cong carried out guerrilla warfare, so operations were impossible without the help of the local population. Therefore, the civil affairs operations aimed at separating the Viet Cong from the local residents were the most important in the Vietnam War. In enemy villages, the Viet Cong hid in the basements of civilian homes. It was a life-risking task to directly enter these areas and conduct operations to persuade the residents. As a result of the success of the Korean military's civil affairs and psychological operations, the local Vietnamese people in the areas where the Korean military was stationed became very friendly.

Combats in Vietnam

After completing a year of service as a platoon leader, I was planning to return home. However, upon hearing that I was proficient in Vietnamese, General Kang Yeong-sik, the Chief of Staff of the Field Army, selected me as his aide-de-camp. In the military, orders are absolute. I had to give up my long-awaited return and extend my service for another year on the Vietnam war.

Rescue operation of children in Donghai village, Ninhoa, Vietnam

Before taking on my new post, I was granted a two week leave to return to Korea. Setting foot on my homeland after such a long time filled me with deep emotion. My mother, overjoyed to see her son safely back from the battlefield, couldn't hide her happiness and even prepared a special meal by slaughtering a hen. Upon returning home, I learned that my beloved younger sister, Cha Jeong-sook, had gotten married to Mr. Cho Chang-rae, a teacher at Deokgok Elementary School. My mother explained that she hadn't informed me because Jeong-sook was getting married before her older brother, and she felt uneasy about that. I felt some regret about missing the wedding of the sister I cherished the most, but I wished the newlyweds a happy life together. Mr. Cho made a good first impression, and I felt at ease believing that he would take good care of Cha Jeong-sook.

The leave passed quickly. Before I knew it, the precious golden days of my leave had ended, and it was time to return to Vietnam war. Soldiers on leave were issued plane tickets back to Vietnam. I went to Gimpo Airfield to board a flight bound for Saigon (Ho Chi Minh City), and my mother insisted on coming with me to the airport to see me off. Carrying in my heart the deep love my mother had for her son, I set off once again for Vietnam war.

In my second year, I was assigned as an aide-de-camp to the Field Army Command, where the working environment was relatively better and I had the opportunity to meet many people. When I was serving in the Civil Affairs and Psychological Operations unit, I struggled because the C-rations supplied by the U.S. military did not suit my taste. However, while working at the Field Army Command, I was able to eat K-rations, which I preferred. K-rations were Korean-style combat meals that included kimchi, beef, and jangjorim, and they suited our palate well.

In Nha Trang, there was a street named "Bacham-dong." Bacham-dong (Ba: three, Cham: hundred, Dong: Vietnamese currency) means three hundred dong. It was a place where our soldiers could satisfy their sexual desires with women for only 300 Vietnamese dong. It was a necessary evil street that fulfilled the sexual desires of young soldiers in a war zone. On weekends, soldiers would line up at "Bacham-dong. In the rooms, there were beds lined up with mosquito nets. While the women chewed gum, looked up at the ceiling, and caught mosquitoes flying around with both palms, the men would finish their business and pass it on to the next person.

Even amid the tragedy of war, the Vietnam War spurred economic development for Korea and provided a valuable opportunity for the Korean military to gain combat experience. The reason Japan was able to rise again from the ashes of World War II was due to the Korean War. By supplying the necessary military goods to the United Nations forces during the Korean War, Japan's economy experienced a rapid surge.

A moment of rest during the Vietnam War (I am on the far right.)

In the same context, the deployment of the Korean military to Vietnam war significantly contributed to South Korea's economic development. Many companies, including construction and transportation firms, expanded into Vietnam and earned foreign currency. Hanjin, the parent company of Korean Air, was able to make substantial profits in the transportation sector due to the Vietnam War. Hyundai Construction and others took a major step forward by constructing the Cam Ranh Air Base. The Korean soldiers sent to Vietnam, in addition to their basic salary from Korea, received dollars under the name of combat allowances, which made a significant contribution to our foreign currency reserves. Most importantly, the Vietnam War played a crucial role in the growth of industries such as Pohang Steel, which served as a driving force behind South Korea's modernization.

During the Vietnam War, we collected shell casings and loaded them onto Navy LST vessels to be transported to Pohang. One of our important tasks during combat in Vietnam was to gather shell casings and send them back to Korea. When soldiers finished their tours and returned home, they would receive three large boxes, fill them with shell casings, and send them to the Pohang Steel Works. As a result, the Vietnam War played a decisive role in raising the South Korean economy to a developed country level.

Shell casings sent to Pohang Steel

Additionally, by providing the South Korean military with

combat experience, the Vietnam War significantly contributed to the enhancement of the military's combat capability. A soldier can only become a true soldier through actual combat experience. The officers and non-commissioned officers of the South Korean military were able to improve their combat effectiveness by participating in the Vietnam War. While enlisted soldiers would discharge after completing their mandatory service, professional soldiers could maintain and strengthen their combat readiness by serving in the military for an extended period.

Nonetheless, there were also side effects. Many of our soldiers who participated in the Vietnam War suffered from the effects of Agent Orange. Vietnam has an average temperature of 34°C and receives about 1,800mm of rainfall annually, making it a dense jungle region.

In order to observe the enemy, herbicides were needed to kill the leaves and grasses, and this herbicide was Agent Orange. It was sprayed by aircraft over the jungle regions and Viet Cong strongholds.

During this process, our soldiers were also affected, and the aftereffects only appeared after a long period of time. The company that produced Agent Orange in the U.S. provided $180 million to fund treatment for Agent Orange victims. The

U.S. government also offered free treatment and sufficient compensation to soldiers who were diagnosed with Agent Orange-related conditions.

Spraying Agent Orange

In Korea, Agent Orange victims became a social issue, and during my time as the Defense Secretary at the Blue House, I helped create a compensation law for Agent Orange victims, similar to the one in the U.S. The law was passed by the National Assembly, and about 10,000 Agent Orange victims received free treatment and compensation from the government. Although the Vietnam War, the first war Korea participated in, brought suffering to veterans due to Agent Orange and other factors, it made a significant contribution to the modernization of South

Korea.

5. The ROK/US Combined Planning Staff

After completing two years of service in Vietnam, I returned to Korea and was assigned to the ROK/US Combined Planning Staff, the predecessor of the ROK/US Combined Forces Command, located in Yongsan, Seoul, before taking on the role of company commander. My time at the ROK/US Combined Planning Staff, situated within the US Eighth Army Command compound, was relatively relaxed. After work, I was able to use my leisure time to attend the master's program at Korea University Graduate School.

The ROK/US Combined Planning Staff was established on October 8, 1968, in Yongsan, Seoul. It was an organization created to facilitate coordinated efforts between the United Nations Command, which held operational control, and the South Korean Joint Chiefs of Staff. Initially, the head of the Combined Planning Staff was a US general. But a South Korean officer took over as the chief of the ROK/US Combined Planning Staff in July 1974, .

Having only served on the front lines and in Vietnam, the environment at the U.S. Eighth Army Command was rather bewildering to me. In the civilian-like atmosphere with regular working hours, I felt a sense of mental and physical lethargy creeping in. After work, rather than wasting time on unnecessary activities, I thought it would be better to study. A colleague, Ms. Kook Young-joo, who graduated from Sookmyung Women's University, was attending a master's program at the graduate school after work. Through her introduction, I enrolled in the master's program at Korea University. Upon starting, I found that Kim Seon-tae, a fellow cadet from the Korean Military Academy and currently working at the Central Intelligence Agency (later National Intelligence Service), was also attending. While I had not had many opportunities to get close to him during our cadet years, we became very close while helping each other during our time in the graduate school.

After work, without even having time for dinner, I would take the bus to Anam-dong, where Korea University was located. Dinner often consisted of ramen and bread during breaks. This was a different master's program from the Executive MBA, so attendance and exams were very strict. Particularly, Professor Kim Haeng-gwon, who supervised my thesis, was known as the 'tiger.' If any cheating was found during the exam, he would take the exam papers on the spot, kick the person out, and give them an F for the course. The discipline here was even stricter than at at the Korea Military Academy. In this environment, I received straight A+'s throughout the entire program and even earned a certificate in international trade.

Master's Degree Conferral at Korea University Graduate School
(From left: Kim Jin, Cha Soo-jin, The Author, Kim Kyeong-ah)

In the last semester when I had to write my master's thesis, I was ordered to go to the front line. In the end, the final thesis was completed after I served as a company commander and worked at the ROK/US Field Army Command, under the guidance of

Professor Kim Haeng-gwon. The title of my thesis was 'A Study on the FMS System (Focusing on the Army's Foreign Procurement).' Earning the master's degree with great difficulty later had a positive impact on my promotions. Furthermore, continuing my studies and earning a PhD eventually helped me become a professor, laying the foundation for my career.

6. Public Proposal and Marriage

While working in Seoul, there were many opportunities for matchmaking. General Kim Jae-myung, the chief of the ROK/US Combined Planning Staff, even tried to introduce me to several young women in an attempt to find me a match. It was also the right time for marriage, so my parents back home were urging me to settle down. However, no one I met sparked my interest.

One day, I received a call from Lieutenant Colonel Cheon Yong-taek (the 16th class of KMA), who worked in the Artillery Department of the Operations Headquarters at the Army Headquarters (later the Minister of Defense and a member of the National Assembly). At that time, the Army Headquarters was located in Yongsan, where the War Memorial stands today. Lieutenant Colonel Cheon told me that a young woman and her mother would be waiting for me at the Dongshim Cafe in Samgakji, and suggested that I meet them.

The background of why Lieutenant Colonel Cheon called me was as follows. My father-in-law, General Kim Seon-gyu (the 2nd class of KMA), had asked Lieutenant Colonel Kim Bong-cheon to publicly recommend a suitable man from the military who could potentially be a son-in-law. LTC Kime was the aide-de-camp of my father in law. LTC Kim, in turn, asked Lieutenant Colonel Cheon, who worked in the same office, to suggest a promising young officer from the Military Academy. Lieutenant Colonel Cheon then got my recommendation from Captain Lee Jae-hwan, my fellow Military Academy classmate, and that's how I ended up being introduced. Captain Lee, who was from the same hometown as Lieutenant Colonel Cheon in Wando, knew LTG Cheon well.

After hearing about it from Lieutenant Colonel Cheon, I went to the Dongshim Cafe in Samgakji, dressed in my work uniform, to meet them. There, I saw a kind-looking middle-aged woman and a beautiful young woman sitting by the window. As soon as our eyes met, I felt an electric spark. I didn't know much about her, but she had already known me through LTC Kim Bong-cheon, so we had a natural conversation while having tea. Her name was Kim Kyeong-ah, and she was studying Childhood Education at Chung-Ang University.

Kim Seon-gyu, my father-in-law, is inspecting the field during the Korean War.

General Kim Seon-gyu, who was to become my father-in-law, was a graduate of the 2nd class of the Korea Military Academy. He served in various important positions, including as the Director of the Communications Department at the Army Headquarters and as the Commander of the 37th Division. During the Korean War, he was a hero of the Battle of Seoraksan in the 21st Division, where he made significant contributions as a commander. Notably, during the Battle of Seoraksan, he repelled an entire enemy battalion and was awarded the Eulji Military Order of Merit, cementing his reputation as a brilliant military leader.

My father-in-law uncle, General Lee Seong-ga, was a war hero who played a crucial role in the Battle of Yeongcheon during the Korean War, where he led the 8th Infantry Division to significant victories. In the Battle of Yeongcheon, he played an essential part in preventing the North Korean forces from capturing Busan, earning a reputation as a heroic leader in the process. My mother-in-law uncle also graduated from the Naval Academy, and my wife's fourth cousin, Kim Jin-hwang, was a graduate of the 28th class of the Korea Military Academy. The family had a strong tradition of military service, and Kim Kyeong-ah, growing up in such an environment, was so devoted to the military that she vowed never to marry anyone who wasn't a soldier. As a result, my father-in-law was specifically looking for a son-in-law from a military background

At the matchmaking meeting at the Dongshim Cafe in Samgakji, the person I met was not unpleasant, but I couldn't easily decide on the life-changing decision of marriage, so I asked for some time. After several more meetings and dates with Kim

Kyeong-ah, we began to understand each other, and I informed my family in Daegu as well. My eldest brother, Cha Ki-whan, visited my in-laws' house in Cheongpa-dong and met with my father-in-law, General Kim Seon-gyu, which led to the wedding preparations moving forward rapidly. On June 6, 1971, we held an engagement ceremony with both families present, and after a walk around the Walkerhill Hotel, we set the wedding date for September 11, 1971. Everything proceeded smoothly and swiftly.

Engagement ceremony
(from left to right: Cha Kyeung-bong, Jeon Soon-seun,
The Author, Kim Kyeong-ah, Kim Sun-gyu)

The master of ceremonies for the engagement ceremony was my classmate from the Korea Military Academy, Captain Kim

Yong-gu. After the ceremony, my classmates, including Captain Lee Jae and Captain Jang Woo-gyun, enjoyed a pleasant time together with my fiancée, Kim Kyeong-ah, while driving around. During the engagement period, my classmates congratulated me on marrying the daughter of a general, and wherever we went, Kim Kyeong-ah's popularity was overwhelming. After the engagement, I received orders to serve as the commander of the 11th Infantry Division's reconnaissance company in Hongcheon. Although I longed to spend more time with my fiancée, I had no choice but to follow the army's orders, leaving behind a bittersweet feeling. The journey from Seoul to Hongcheon felt incredibly heavy, as if every step was laden with reluctance.

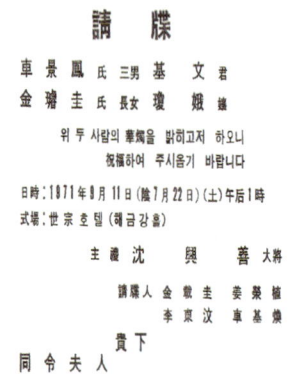

Wedding chest delivery: my KMA classmate Kim Kwang-su carries the chest, guided by classmates Kim Yong-gu and On Chang-il, holding traditional lanterns

The reconnaissance company of the division was larger than a regular infantry company and had equipment such as the company commander's personal jeep and a five-minute standby trucks always on standby. The company had its own PX and was a completely independent unit with its own cooking facilities. As I was assigned as the company commander and continued with my busy schedule, the wedding date was gradually approaching.

Wedding at the Sejong Hotel

On September 10, the day before the wedding, I changed from my combat uniform into formal attire and headed to Seoul to attend the ceremony held at the Sejong Hotel, my face darkly tanned from field duty. That evening, the wedding chest was delivered, and the narrow alleys of Cheongpa-dong, where my fiancée's family lived, were bustling with the arrival of many of my KMA classmates. On Chang-il and Kim Yong-gu led the way, holding traditional lanterns and blowing horns. When Kim Kwang-su, who had married early and already had a son, carried the wedding chest, the entire neighborhood turned into a festive scene.

The officiant was General Shim Heung-seon, who was serving as Chairman of the Joint Chiefs of Staff, and the master of ceremonies was my classmate Lee Jae from the Korea Military Academy, studying Korean literature at Seoul National University. Lee Jae's witty hosting and General Shim Heung-seon's seasoned officiating created a solemn and warmly congenial atmosphere.

Honeymoon in Jeju Island

After the wedding, we left for our honeymoon in Jeju Island, receiving warm farewells from our families. At the time, most newlyweds went to Jeju for their honeymoon, as it was rare for people to travel abroad. I had visited Jeju once during my cadet days with my classmate Kim Moon-gi, but seeing Jeju again on my honeymoon gave me an entirely different feeling. After landing at Jeju Airport, we rented a car and toured the coast as we made our way to Seogwipo. We spent our first night at the Honeymoon House in Seogwipo and, surrounded by the tropical atmosphere of Jeju, we forgot about military duties and enjoyed time just for the two of us. Following the honeymoon itinerary, we lost track of time in happiness.

According to traditional Korean customs, newlyweds were expected to hold a wedding feast at the groom's family home after returning from their honeymoon. After coming back from Jeju Island, we spent one night at my in-laws' house and then traveled to my hometown, Deoksilgol in Hapcheon, for the wedding visit. On the way to my hometown via Daegu, my father-in-law, mother-in-law, and brother-in-law Kim Jin accompanied us.

The journey from Seoul to Daegu took four hours; from Daegu to Deoksilgol, it took another two hours. At the Nakdong

River ferry terminal, the car was loaded onto a boat to cross the river, and after traveling on a long stretch of unpaved country roads, we finally arrived at Deoksilgol. When we arrived, my wife's family seemed visibly disappointed. No cultural facilities were in sight, just a traditional outhouse, thatched roofs with chilies drying, and children gathering around as the car pulled into the village. However, the warm kindness and love of the humble people, which I hadn't seen in Seoul, seemed somewhat comforting.

My farther and mother rejoice
after receiving the wedding feast

Eldest brother and his spouse
the three sisters, wife, and the author

My father and mother had slaughtered cows and pigs to prepare a large feast and were waiting for us. It was clear they were very pleased to have their youngest son bring his beautiful bride from Seoul for the wedding celebration. Such a rare event in the countryside meant even the peddlers from ten miles away showed up. The villagers spent the whole day enjoying themselves, playing traditional Korean music, eating, and drinking.

I couldn't stay long in the village, as I had recently taken up the position of company commander and had to return to my unit quickly. My father and mother seemed to want me to stay a little longer, but bound by military duties, I only stayed one night in my hometown before heading back to my unit in Hongcheon.

Upon returning to Hongcheon, my newlywed wife and I began our married life in a shabby, isolated house standing alone in the fields. Fortunately, my senior classmates from the Korea Military Academy, Shin Jeong and Hong Yoo-kyung, and their families, lived nearby, providing some comfort during my newlywed days.

7. Being a Company Commander and Newlywed

After being assigned as the commander of the reconnaissance company in the division, I was fully committed to making my company the best unit in the division. Even though my wife and I were newlyweds, I spent more time at the unit than at home. The 11th Division, nicknamed the "Hwarang Division," was the mobile division in the field army and was tasked with performing counteroffensive missions across the entire theater of operations, making it a unit with rigorous training. The mobile division is likened to a fire truck, as it must be deployed anywhere in times of emergency. For this reason, the 11th Division was located in Hongcheon, which had a well-developed transportation network.

To carry out immediate mobility missions, the 11th Division conducted frequent marches. Soldiers dreaded being assigned to the 11th Division because they were often told they would have to walk the equivalent of three times around the Earth before they could be discharged. However, once assigned, the training forged a strong bond of camaraderie, and this affection for the unit turned soldiers into those who cried when they joined, but left smiling. With its long history and tradition, the soldiers of the legendary Hwarang Division sang the division song at the top of their lungs to the sound of the military band, their morale soaring sky-high.

I aimed to further enhance the tradition of the unit, which had the soul embedded in the division song, as soon as I was assigned as the commander of the reconnaissance company. I immediately began day-night transition training. The training involved switching between night and day activities. For a month, we trained through the night and slept during the day. To turn the soldiers into experts in nighttime combat, I conducted "owl training." The company members endured this training well. Although there were difficulties at first due to the adjustment, they gradually became more proficient and gained confidence, evolving into an "owl unit" specialized in nighttime combat.

My wife, Kim Kyeong-ah,
at the reconnaissance company commander's quarters

My newlywed wife was not accustomed to rural life and said

she was scared to stay alone in the mountain house at night. My house, located in the desolate plains where the wind howled, was a traditional home with a fireplace where meals were cooked with firewood. At night, the area would become eerily quiet, with only the sounds of wild animals echoing through the air, and there wasn't a single trace of human presence in the mountain village.

Leaving my young bride alone at night in such a remote mountain home weighed heavily on my mind. However, as the company commander responsible for the lives of 180 soldiers, the unit had to come before family. I had no choice but to dedicate all my time and energy to unit training, putting the soldiers before my own home.

After my wife became pregnant, she was stoking the fire in the kitchen hearth when a rat suddenly jumped out. Startled, she fainted and had to be rushed to the hospital for emergency treatment, but sadly, she lost the baby. After that incident, she began suffering frequent miscarriages due to severe bleeding, which became a chronic condition. This was why our first daughter, Suj-in, was born much later.

When we ran low on firewood, we would go to the mountains and collect rotting tree stumps and bundles of pine needles for heating. During the cold winter, we once burned so much firewood that the floor near the furnace overheated, nearly causing a fire. Since the house lacked proper insulation, the floor would cool quickly, and by dawn, the water bowls placed at the far end of the room would be frozen solid. Sometimes, rats would fall from the ceiling while fighting among themselves. Even in such harsh conditions, my wife never once complained and gave her full support to her husband, the company commander, for which I was deeply grateful.

Once, a soldier in my company asked for leave, saying that his girlfriend had had a change of heart. It was evident that, if granted leave, he might act out and do something reckless to her. At the time, there had been many cases of soldiers in similar situations going into civilian areas with grenades, harming random people, or taking hostages. When I denied his request, he came to the company commander's quarters wielding a sharp knife and causing a commotion. In the end, I got in touch with his girlfriend and carefully reasoned with the soldier to help him understand. After that, I granted him leave, and he eventually became a model soldier.

After the reconnaissance company won the sports competition

sister-in-law, mother-in-law, wife, brother-in-law

In winter, an ice skating competition was held along the Hongcheon River. The soldiers eagerly awaited the winter when they could skate. The Hongcheon River became a great training ground during the winter after being blocked in late autumn. Our company consistently won the competitions between units. We held a company dinner when we won a pig as a prize, which boosted the soldiers' morale. My brother-in-law and sister-in-law loved skating, so on weekends, my wife's family from Seoul would come to visit. My wife eagerly awaited such weekends, enduring life at the front.

Occasionally, my wife's friends would visit my home to support their newlywed friend. One of my wife's university friends, Shin Jeong-ja, a beautiful single woman, frequently visited the country house to support my wife. One day, my classmate from the Korea Military Academy, Captain Kim Yong-kyung, also serving as a company commander in a neighboring unit, came to our house and met her. The two felt an immediate connection. Captain Kim, a sturdy man who played Rugby at the Korea Military Academy, was kind-hearted and caring. Thanks to my wife's enthusiastic matchmaking, the two eventually married, and our two families maintained a bond so strong that it felt like we were blood relatives for the rest of our lives.

From the left, my family, Captain Shin's, and Captain Hong's

Next to our house in the countryside of Hongcheon, Captain Shin Jeong and Captain Hong Yu-kyung's family (the 20th class of the Korea Military Academy), lived together. Captain Shin's wife graduated from Korea University, and Captain Hong's wife graduated from Ewha Womans University, so they all had much in common. We would play tennis together, and in the summer, my wife and they would go to the Hongcheon Riverbank to do the laundry, easing the loneliness of life in the countryside.

Our reconnaissance company participated in the 13th Regiment's RCT (Regimental Combat Team) exercises. The 13th Regiment, commanded by Colonel Ahn Jae-seok, a graduate of the 11th class of the Korea Military Academy, was known to be the best regiment in the field army. To verify if this reputation was deserved, General Han Shin, the field army commander, personally flew in by helicopter and conducted an unannounced evaluation of the regimental combat team exercise. Our reconnaissance company was assigned to participate in this test.

The training took place along Route 44, which runs from Hongcheon to Inje. During the march, a situation was suddenly created in which we encountered a powerful enemy, and the commanders' response was assessed. As enemy tanks focused on breaking through, the regiment faced the prospect of total collapse. The unit's soldiers, unable to find their parent unit, were in disarray, and the commanders were busy trying to reorganize their units.

Enemy tank units had already occupied the road, so our company had to infiltrate toward the target area via mountain trails. During the infiltration, we suffered heavy casualties from enemy ambushes, and by the time we reached the final objective, only half of our forces remained.

Under these harsh conditions, while most of the units were utterly wiped out, our company regrouped and struck at the enemy's rear command post despite being reduced to half of its original strength. Then, the 13th Regiment captured the final objective, and the regimental combat teams received a successful evaluation. During the debriefing, General Han Shin, the commanding general of the field army, praised our company. Our reconnaissance company was recognized as the best unit in the entire army. As a result of this training, Colonel Ahn Jae-seok, the commander of the 13th Regiment, highly evaluated our company, and I developed a strong personal bond with Colonel Ahn.

8. The Tearful Farewell Ceremony of the Company Commander

A company commander is a position where the leader

directly interacts with their subordinates, feeling the most affection and love from them. A platoon leader also interacts directly with subordinates, but a platoon leader is a leader, not a commander. A battalion commander is also a commander, yet they lead and control the unit through the advice of staff officers and lower-level commanders like company commanders. As a result, battalion commanders have fewer opportunities for direct interaction with their subordinates. A company commander holds immense authority and responsibility as the unit commander with operational and administrative authority. The company commander has the authority and responsibility to feed, clothe, and shelter the soldiers. I knew the names of all 180 members of my company. I could recognize a soldier just by the way they walked from behind. If I called out a soldier's name while walking down the road, the soldier would be surprised that the company commander recognized them and would instinctively feel respect. Since I thoroughly understood each soldier's situation, asking about their family matters further strengthened their loyalty.

However, it is not enough to treat soldiers with kindness alone. Those who violate regulations must be held accountable, and I administered penalties with such strictness that they were almost brought to tears.

The reconnaissance company

After the punishment, if I saw genuine remorse, I would privately call them to offer warm encouragement as part of the follow-up process, providing relief and support. Only then could they truly reflect on their actions and develop respect for the company commander. By rewarding those who followed the rules and did good deeds, I encouraged others to do the same. When awarding a prize, I gathered all the company members on the parade ground and held a grand ceremony. Exemplary soldiers should be recognized publicly. The recipient also felt pride and a sense of achievement, and recognizing them in front of many people amplified the effect. When administering punishment, I did it quietly and privately. Punishment could bring shame to subordinates, so it was better to handle it discreetly. Since people are emotional beings, if emotions are heightened, they may not even recognize their mistakes and instead may resist, leading to bigger problems. Therefore, awards should be public, while punishments should be individual to achieve better results.

Officers of the reconnaissance company

Soldiers in a company are a diverse group from all over the country. They have different personalities, hobbies, thoughts, and behaviors. It is not easy to unify this mixed group into a cohesive unit capable of achieving victory in combat. In our neighboring units, some soldiers deserted, and some even committed suicide. Under such circumstances, the role of the company commander, who must manage the unit without any safety losses while training it to become a group capable of fighting and defeating the enemy in battle, is truly significant. A company commander must possess wisdom, determination, and strong practical ability as a manager and leader. Continuous self-discipline, tactical knowledge, and physical strength are required to cultivate this wisdom and ability.

Leading a unit requires, above all, love and affection. A company commander must set aside personal interests and dedicate everything solely to the unit and the soldiers. During my tenure as the company commander, I take pride in the fact that our unit did not experience a single suicide or armed desertion, which I believe was a result of my leadership to this day. Our reconnaissance company was selected as the division's vanguard unit through successful unit management and morale-boosting training that emulated actual combat. All the soldiers in our company were confident, believing they could fight and defeat the enemy even if war broke out that night. This confidence became evident when the division conducted combat readiness assessments and competitions. We consistently received awards and won in tactical knowledge contests and sports competitions.

At the end of my two-year term as company commander, all the soldiers could not hold back their sadness at our parting. The farewell ceremony was filled with tears. I choked up during my farewell speech and, unable to continue, broke down in tears. The soldiers, too, without exception, were in tears. Such experiences are a privilege unique to a company commander.

9. To the Officer Advanced Course

After completing my term as a company commander, I entered the Officer Advanced Course (OAC) for infantry in Gwangju. The military provides refresher training courses at each rank. When one is assigned as a platoon leader, they take the Officer Basic Course (OBC); before becoming a company commander, the Officer Advanced Course; before becoming a battalion commander, the Army College; and before becoming a regimental commander, the National Defense Graduate School. The training system was not yet fully established, so I entered the Officer Advanced Course after completing my service as a company commander.

I visited Gwangju for the third time—first during my third year at the Korea Military Academy for branch training, then as a newly commissioned second lieutenant for the Officer Basic Course, and now again for the Officer Advanced Course. It was a welcome reunion to see my classmates who had served in each units after completing the Officer Basic Course and returned to Gwangju for the Officer Advanced Course. The Korea Military Academy cadets spend 24 hours a day together, forming bonds like brothers. Even after graduation, we continued to encounter one another through training programs and assignments. With so many shared experiences throughout our lives, we remained lifelong comrades, closer than any other kind of peer. The Officer Advanced Course had a significant impact on promotion and future assignments, so we studied through the night. Everyone was so dedicated that even short breaks felt like a waste of time. If we had studied law with the same intensity we applied to the Officer Advanced Course, we probably could have easily passed the bar exam.

Since I had a wife when I entered the 19th OAC class, we had to find a place to live in Gwangju. Finding a room in Gwangju was not easy. While searching for a place, I had my wife stay at her parents' home in Seoul and went to Gwangju alone, where I boarded at the home of my classmate Han Gwang-so, originally from Gwangju. Han's parents had great affection for our classmates and took devoted care of those of us who came to Gwangju.

So many classmates wanted to board live in Hans' house, but not everyone could be accommodated. Some classmates had to stay at a neighboring house known for having many daughters. This "house full of daughters" in Gwangju was so well known that there wasn't a single officer entering the Officer's Advanced Course who hadn't heard of it. This house even had a traditional collection of Officer's Advanced Course exam questions from previous tests, known as the Jeonggamnok. The Jeonggamnok was a compilation of questions passed down from seniors who had studied there. Many of the actual test questions were taken from that compilation, which was extremely helpful for preparing for the Officer's Advanced Course exams.

I stayed at Han Gwang-so parents' home for a month before finally renting a room in Hwanggeum-dong, Gwangju, and bringing my wife from Seoul. Hwanggeum-dong was a neighborhood packed with bars, making it far from ideal for studying, but since it was so challenging to find a place, I had no choice but to rent a room in one of the alleys lined with bars. When I studied past midnight, drunk people would roam around outside, causing a commotion. A barmaid lived in the room next to mine, and she would often bring men back late at night to continue drinking. Since the walls were not well insulated, I could even hear her urinating into a chamber pot, which made it all the more distracting. Still, recalling the ascetic training of *Seosan Daesa* (a renowned Korean Buddhist monk from the 16th century, known for his deep meditation and teachings in the Zen tradition), I did not let these conditions shake my determination to study; instead, I focused all the more intensely on my studies.

There were also many officers in the Officer's Advance Course who joined my junior of the military academy. Many of them came to our house, where my wife would cook for them, and we would study together. Among them was Captain Lee Han-eok, a 25th graduate of the Korea Military Academy. My wife arranged a match for him with her cousin on her mother's side. After graduating from the Officer's Advanced Course, their love grew deeper, and they eventually married, becoming a happy couple.

I never slept more than 2~3 hours a day during the Officer's Advance Course. Without a single day off, I was fully absorbed in reviewing and preparing lessons. There was no time to enjoy newlywed life. I even continued studying while eating or using the bathroom. That level of dedication enabled me to graduate at the top of my class. I was honored with the Chief of Staff of the Army Award, which had a significant impact on my military career, and received congratulations from many. I cannot emphasize enough how crucial my wife's support was to this achievement. She ensured I received proper nutrition by going all the way to the traditional market to buy high-protein fish. She even sealed the door gaps with traditional paper for soundproofing to create a better study environment. She truly helped shape a pivotal moment in my career.

19th OAC Class (I am seated third from the left in the front row.)

After completing the Officer Advanced Course at the Infantry School, I felt confident enough to assume the role of a division commander immediately. I believed I could achieve any given mission with 100% success, as if the world were in my palm. I had more confidence than anyone in the field of tactics, and the distinction of graduating at the top of my class remained on my service record throughout my career.

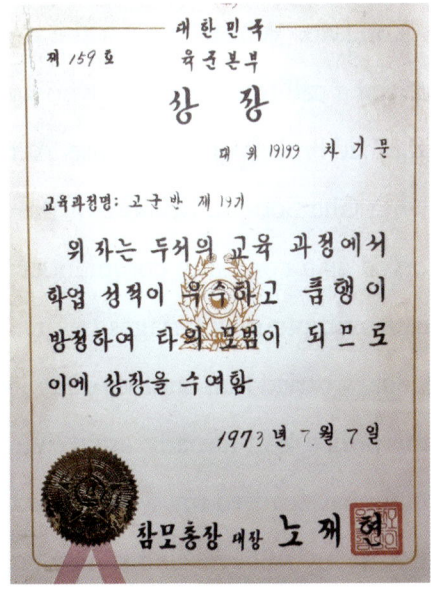

Award from the Chief of Staff of the Army for the OAC

Whenever I was assigned to a new unit, commanders would compete to bring me into their own. Graduating at the top of the

Officer Advanced Course had a significant impact on the smooth progress of my military career. After completing the course, I was assigned to a unit in the capital area. Having mostly served in front-line units and Vietnam war, I was given an opportunity to serve in the rear according to the rotational assignment system. Due to a shortage of military apartments, one had to wait a long time to move in, even after receiving a transfer order, so my mother-in-law and wife found a two-story townhouse in Seobinggo, Yongsan. While I was at the unit during a busy workday, I received a call from my wife, who was home alone—she said a burglar had broken into the house. At the time, my wife was pregnant with Cha Soo-jin. Because of the harsh conditions when I had served as a company commander at the front, she had experienced multiple miscarriages before conceiving Soo-jin, so I was deeply worried that another one might occur. When I got home, the police had already apprehended the burglar. Thinking he might have caused my wife to miscarry, I kicked the seated burglar with my military boots. The burglar passed out on the spot, and I ended up being summoned by the police to be questioned on charges of assault.

Later, I found out that it was my wife who had caught the burglar. As she returned home from the market and entered the house, she came face to face with the intruder in the living room. She struck him with the shopping basket she was carrying, and in a panic, the burglar jumped out of the second-floor window. He fell through the roof of a nearby shack. My wife, along with some neighbors, chased him down and handed him over to the police. Perhaps that moment of bravery was passed on to our unborn child, because Cha Soo-jin was born with a strong resilience as if she could thrive even in the harshest conditions.

Chapter 2

●

| The Years as a Field Officer |

1. The Cradle of Military Education
   : ROK Army College

After being promoted to major, I attended the Republic of Korea Army College to receive the education required of a senior officer. At the time, the college was located at the foot of Mount Cheonja in Jinhae. Jinhae is a naval port city, and in spring, it becomes a beautiful harbor filled with blooming cherry blossoms and crowds of tourists. With its harmonious blend of mountains and sea, Jinhae was like a paradise for military families. They enjoyed tennis, badminton, fishing, and hiking in the clean air and clear water of the scenic harbor city. But for officers who had to devote themselves to studying day and night, it was also a kind of hell.

The Republic of Korea Army College, known as the cradle of strategy and tactics, was famous for its rigorous academic requirements. School performance was directly tied to promotions and assignments, so everyone put in their best effort to achieve the best grades. Admission to the Republic of Korea Army College was not easy. At the time, there were two course: the regular course, which lasted one year, and the short-term course, which was a six-month program. The one-year regular course had a competitive ratio of 30 to 1. Around the Army Headquarters, where the exams were held, people were studying together in camps to be admitted to the regular course. When I was about to enter the Republic of Korea Army College, I lived in a military apartment in the Haebangchon area of Yongsan, Seoul. Though it was only about 29.7 square meters in size and didn't even have a living room, it was a sturdy house built with the first military materials in Korea. Despite having a coal boiler, it was well-heated and well-ventilated, making it convenient to live in. To move into this apartment, I had to wait in line for several months even after receiving an assignment.

I was lucky to move into the Haebangchon military apartment relatively quickly; at that time, Sujin was still an infant. I did my best to study in that small apartment to enter the Republic of Korea Army College, and as a result, I was accepted as the youngest person to graduate at the top of my class. Everyone else was a major or lieutenant colonel, but only four captains, including me, were admitted to the Republic of Korea Army College. The others were my fellow cadets from the 23rd class of the Korea Military Academy: No Nam-seop, Yoo Jae-hyun, and Jeong Hwa-eon.

I entered the ROK Army College as part of the 19th class in 1975 and graduated in 1976. Among my fellow cadets from the 23rd class of the Korea Military Academy, the four of us who entered the Republic of Korea Army College first were assigned to the lowest-ranking C barracks. The C barracks were located at the foot of Cheonjasan Mountain and consisted of townhouses, where coal gas would leak, leaving the rooms constantly smelling of gas. When we opened the door, the ground was right there, and when it rained, it became a muddy mess. Fortunately, there was an open lot in front of the house where we could grow vegetables. In the spring, I shared the joy of planting seeds and growing vegetables with the neighboring officers, which helped maintain good relationships. When you live together in difficult conditions, the bond of comradeship becomes even stronger. The four of us who went through the tough process at the the Republic of Korea Army College became like a close family during our military service.

The Republic of Korea Army College in Jinhae

The four of us, the youngest in the class, had to serve as the class aides, responsible for running errands. Since our ranks were low, we had no opportunities to interact with the instructors. The instructors were all senior officers, and the senior class members could interact with the instructors and even get hints about the direction of the exams. However, the four of us had no choice but to focus entirely on studying. We stayed up all night studying and spent most of our free time in the library. The exams lasted for 8 hours straight. The questions involved analyzing the situation, providing maps, and creating division and corps-level operational plans. The problem required us to devise a plan on how the allied forces would operate to fight and win against the enemy. After sitting through the 8-hour exam without even being able to go to the bathroom, we were almost on the verge of collapsing.

At that time, there were students at the Republic of Korea Army College who lost their lives while studying. One officer, who lived in the house next door, collapsed over his desk while studying for the exam and was found as a cold, lifeless body. Despite having a cold, he had not properly managed his health and continued studying for the exam the next day. It was diagnosed that he had overdosed on medicine while pushing himself too hard, staying up all night, and ultimately lost his life.

The support of wives was one of the most important factors while the husbands were studying. While studying, their appetite would decrease, and digestion would become difficult. The stress inevitably led to poor health. Military families would go to Jinhae Market to buy high-protein fish, such as eel and catfish, and feed them to their husbands. If there were anything that could help with studying, they would go as far as Masan, across the mountains, to buy it, showing their extreme dedication.

Below Cheonjabong, there was a spring called Dobuljang. Every morning, I would go there to drink spring water and hike as part of my health routine. Climbing the mountain itself was exercise, and breathing in the fresh morning air refreshed my mind and greatly helped with my studies. The dewy, narrow path leading to the spring was quite romantic. Frogs would line up along the way, and when a person passed by, they would scatter to the side of the path all at once.

Awarded the Minister of National Defense Award

I achieved excellent academic results while focusing on strategic and tactical studies and maintaining my health with early morning hikes. Upon graduation, I was awarded the Minister of National Defense Award. Since I had entered the Republic of Korea Army College as the top student, the sense of responsibility to maintain that level of performance led me to receive this prestigious honor. After our group of four, many classmates followed suit the following year.

On July 19, 1976, after graduating from the Republic of Korea Army College, I was assigned to the U.S./ROK Combined I Corps in Uijeongbu. From then on, I was confident in strategic and tactical matters as a senior officer. I felt that I could take on roles such as the Minister of National Defense or Chief of Staff of the Army with ease. The excellent results from the Republic of Korea Army College also played a key role in my later opportunity to attend the U.S. Command and General Staff College, which goes without saying.

2. Operations Officer of the ROK/US Combined 1st Corps and the 8.18 Hatchet Massacre

I was assigned as the operations officer of the ROK/US Combined 1st Corps and became the primary officer responsible for drafting the western front defense plan for Operation Plan 5027. It was during this time that the August 18 Hatchet Massacre occurred. On August 18, 1976, at around 10:30 AM, 15 guards and laborers were cutting branches of a mulberry tree in the Joint Security Area of Panmunjom, which obstructed the view of a South guard post. North Korean officer Park Cheol arrived with his subordinates and ordered them to stop the trimming. U.S. Army officer Captain Arthur Bonifas ignored the order and instructed the workers to continue. He was a West Point graduate, with only three days left in his one-year assignment in Korea. Park Cheol called for additional North Korean troops. Over 30 North Korean soldiers arrived by truck, carrying iron rods and axes. They surrounded the laborers who were trimming the branches. Park Cheol again demanded that the work stop. As Captain Bonifas turned his back, ignoring the order, Park Cheol took off his wristwatch, wrapped it in a handkerchief, and put it in his pocket. He shouted, "Kill him!" and struck Captain Bonifas in the neck, knocking him down.

At the same time, North Korean soldiers attacked the UN guard and laborers. Captain Bonifas was struck with iron rods and axes and was killed instantly at the scene. U.S. Army officer Lieutenant Mark Barrett, who was nearby, was also killed by an axe while attempting to manage the situation. One South Korean officer and four soldiers, along with four U.S. soldiers, were injured. By the time the UN mobile strike force arrived, the North Korean soldiers had already crossed the Military

Demarcation Line.

8.18 Hatchet Massacre

When this news reached Washington, President Gerald Ford was attending the Republican National Convention in Kansas City, where he was receiving criticism from Ronald Reagan for being too soft on communism. The National Security Council convened in Washington. In an emergency security meeting, it was first decided to send additional troops to Korean Peninsula. Phantom squadrons were to be moved from the Okinawa base to Korea Peninsula, and F-111 bombers from Idaho were also to be sent to Korea Peninsula. B-52 strategic bombers stationed in Guam were to be sent to fly over the Korean Demilitarized Zone, and the Midway aircraft carrier fleet in Japan was to be moved to the East Sea. Shocked by the gravity of its reckless actions, North Korea immediately went on a combat readiness alert. A curfew was enforced in Pyongyang, and key figures took shelter in underground bunkers. North Korean forces on the front lines were put on full alert. The South Korean military and U.S. forces in Korea raised their alert to DEFCON III and entered a state of emergency.

On August 20, 1976, General Stilwell, the U.N Commander, went to the Blue House and reported the retaliation plan to President Park Chung-hee from 11:00 AM for 45 minutes. He stated, "Our forces will enter the Joint Security Area and cut down the problematic mulberry tree. If North Korean forces launch a counterattack, we will immediately respond with force, cross the Military Demarcation Line, recapture Kaesong, and advance deep into the Yeonbaek Plain to address the proximity of the western front to the capital, Seoul." After receiving this report, President Park Chung-hee responded, "The military operation should be limited to cutting down the mulberry tree, and we should only escalate if North Korea escalates. We cannot remain passive, even thought the Joint Security Area is under U.N. control. the South Korean military should handle the tasks of cutting, security, while U.S. forces should handle the second line."[1]

Following these strategic directives, I, in charge of the operational planning for the ROK/U.S. Combined 1st Corps, began drafting the specific operation plan. I established a detailed plan to deploy the 1st Airborne Brigade of the South Korean Army to cut down the mulberry tree. During the operation, the 1st Division was to be deployed in advance to prepare for any unforeseen circumstances. Air Force fighter jets and bombers were to remain on standby in the air. The U.S. 7th Fleet was also instructed to take up a firing posture in the Yellow Sea.

Deployment of U.S. strategic assets during the 8.18 Hatchet Massacre

---

1 Park Hee-do, *Standing on the Bridge of No Return* (Seoul: Samteo, 1988), pp. 103-105.

On August 21, 1976, around 04:00 AM, 64 commandos, consisting of South Korean airborne soldiers, were awaiting deployment in a gymnasium within the 2nd U.S. Infantry Division. These commandos were elite soldiers selected from the 1st Airborne Brigade. They were instructed to hide their weapons. Wearing bulletproof vests and helmets without rank insignia, the commandos boarded three trucks, carrying only clubs (pickaxe handles). For self-defense, pistols and grenades were concealed inside their bulletproof vests, as carrying weapons was in violation of the regulations within the Joint Security Area.

The special forces troops arrived at the Kitty Hawk Camp, the forward base for the Joint Security Area, which was later renamed Bonifas Camp in honor of the U.S. Army captain who was killed during the August 18 Hatchet Massacre. At 07:00 AM that day, 23 convoy vehicles entered the Joint Security Area without prior notification to the North Korean side. Sixteen engineers began cutting down the mulberry tree with chainsaws and axes. They also dismantled two barricades that the North Koreans had arbitrarily set up within the Joint Security Area. South Korean special forces provided security for the operation. In the sky, 20 UH-1H helicopters and 7 Cobra attack helicopters were circling with a loud noise. Above, a squadron of B-52 bombers, loaded with bombs, was circling under the protection of fighter jets. At Osan, a heavily armed squadron of F-111 bombers was on standby. At sea, the Midway aircraft carrier fleet was in position, and along the Military Demarcation Line, all soldiers had their fingers on the triggers.[2]

A command headquarters to oversee this operation was established in the underground bunker operations control room of the ROK/U.S. Combined 1st Corps, where I was stationed. Following this scenario, I was in charge of coordinating all combat elements, hoping that the mulberry tree would be successfully cut down. At 07:22, while the tree was being cut with chainsaws, approximately 200 North Korean soldiers were seen approaching from the direction of the Bridge of No Return. However, they did not cross the bridge and only took photographs, merely watching until 07:42, when the mulberry tree was completely cut down and fell.

At that time, Major General Han Ju-kyung, the North Korean senior representative to the Military Armistice Commission, requested a secret meeting with the UN senior representative to

---

2   Kim Sang-woong, *A Concise History of Post-Liberation Korea* (Seoul: Garam Planning, 1999), pp. 85–90.

deliver a personal letter from Kim Il-sung. It was the first time Kim Il-sung had written to the United Nations Command. The letter expressed regret. The UNC interpreted it as an apology.

The successful completion of the concluding operation related to the August 18 Hatchet Massacre was thanks to the flawless ROK/U.S. combined operation. In particular, the effective integration of ROK/U.S. operational elements developed by the ROK/U.S. Combined 1st Corps demonstrated that successful operations could be carried out in response to any provocation. After this operation, the need for a command structure for ROK/U.S. combined operations was raised. From that point forward, discussions for establishing the ROK/U.S. Combined Forces Command began in earnest, and on November 7, 1978, the ROK/U.S. Combined Forces Command was established in Yongsan.

3. Studying at the U.S. Army Command and General Staff College

The English I had learned while serving alongside U.S. soldiers in the ROK/U.S. Combined 1st Corps, along with the

Minister of National Defense Award I received upon graduating from the Republic of Korea Army College, laid the foundation for my admission to the U.S. Army Command and General Staff College. The U.S. Army Command and General Staff College is the army college of the United States. Graduating from this institution puts one at a significant advantage in military service, so competition for admission was intense. After overcoming many competitors and being accepted, I traveled to the United States for the first time in my life on June 27, 1977. I departed for study abroad in the U.S. from Gimpo Airport, seeing off my wife, Cha Soo-jin, and mother-in-law. The officers who went with me were Major Kang Seung-gil and Major Noh Dong-jun, both my classmates from the Korea Military Academy, Major Kim Man-taek from the 24th class of the Korea Military Academy, and Marine Corps Lieutenant Colonel Shin Jung-cheol.

The U.S. Army Command and General Staff College, located at Fort Leavenworth in the state of Kansas, is a prestigious institution with a long-standing tradition and history alongside the U.S. Army. Since only selected officers in the United States are admitted to this school, U.S. Army officers chosen for this program often refer to it as "The Best Year of My Life."

Leaders from countries around the world have passed through

this school. In Korea, many of the key military commanders are graduates of this institution, making it a school that every career military officer aspires to attend at least once. In 1977, the year I entered, over 100 foreign officers selected from around the world studied alongside more than 1,000 U.S. Army officers. The class was divided into 22 sections, each consisting of 56 officers, totaling 1,232 students. I was assigned to Section 14, where officers like Colonel Emanuel Sakal from Israel, Lieutenant Colonel Alberto Moreno from Nicaragua, Major Bjarne Hesselberg from Denmark, and Major Jaouadi Abdelaziz from Tunisia were placed together with U.S. Army officers.

Wargame exercise at the U.S. Army Command and General Staff College
(From left: Ron Green, Emanuel Sakal, and the author)

Foreign officers were each assigned a sponsor composed of U.S. Army officers and civilians. My sponsor was a U.S. Army lieutenant colonel named R.C. Ragland, who was also a businessman living in Kansas City. Lieutenant Colonel Ragland's wife was Korean, and they were a happily married couple with six daughters. He took me to his home and introduced me to his family. All six daughters, born to his Korean wife, had a deep interest in Korea and were living happily in a warm and harmonious family atmosphere.

The Volkswagen we purchased

The first thing I did was purchase a vehicle. Unlike in Korea, in the United States, it is virtually impossible to get around without a car. The campus was so large that we had to drive to attend academic activities. Since I didn't have enough money, I couldn't afford a new car, so I bought a used German-made Volkswagen. Major Kang Seung-gil suggested that we share the car, so we bought a yellow Volkswagen shaped like a beetle and used it well until the end of the course.

Golf course in the U.S. Army Command and General Staff College

Within the campus, there was a 18-hole golf course. As the school had a long-standing tradition, the course was surrounded by large trees, and just looking out over the field gave a refreshing sense of openness. It was here that Mrs. Ragland taught me how to play golf. Since I had already graduated from the Republic of

Korea Army College in Korea, the curriculum at the U.S. Army Command and General Staff College, which was similarly structured, was not a burden for me.

A day at the U.S. Army Command and General Staff College BOQ

Above all, the most difficult issue was meals. Since I was living in the BOQ (Bachelor Officers' Quarters), I usually ate Western food at the officers' mess located on the lower floor. Craving Korean food, I went to the supermarket to buy rice, meat, and vegetables and cooked meals myself at the BOQ. Colonel Hua Ming Shuai, a Chinese officer in the room next to mine, taught me how to cook. In China, it is common for men to cook, and his cooking skills were exceptional. He showed me how to make a dish by boiling beef bones—which were relatively inexpensive because Americans didn't eat them much—to make a rich broth, then adding vegetables and meat. I felt as if I had become a master chef.

While cooking for myself, I often craved kimchi. I wrote a letter to my wife in Korea and learned how to make kimchi from her instructions. Following the directions she wrote in the letter, I salted the napa cabbage and left it to soak while I went on an academic field trip. After class, I returned and added the seasoning to the salted cabbage to make the kimchi, but the result was inedible—the cabbage had become mushy like it had been boiled and was too salty and bitter to eat. I had left the cabbage in the salt for too long, and it had broken down. I realized that making kimchi was the most difficult among all the cooking tasks. In the end, I had no choice but to give up on the kimchi I had so badly wanted to eat.

As the school curriculum allowed for some spare time, I had the opportunity to introduce Korean culture to Americans. I gave lectures related to Korea at places like the Rotary Club in Kansas City. I also opened Korean language and Korean studies classes for U.S. and allied officers and their families, which gained great popularity.

I was deeply impressed by the military spirit of "eternal

battlefield readiness" shown by Israeli armored forces Colonel Emanuel Sakal, who was in the same section as me. They had no concept of work uniforms, dress uniforms, or ceremonial uniforms—only combat uniforms. He wore his combat uniform during class, to parties, and even on holidays. All of their thoughts and actions were directly tied to combat readiness. During class, he shared his experiences from the Middle East war in front of all the students. His practical and real-life presentation received enthusiastic applause from all of us.

With Lieutenant Colonel Kuroyanagi from Japan (I am on the right)

One foreign officer I was especially close to was Lieutenant Colonel Kuroyanagi Teruhisa from Japan. He came with his family and often invited me to his home, as I was living alone in the BOQ. Whenever we went to Kansas or Missouri City, we would drive together, engaging in discussions about the Northeast Asian political situation, which helped strengthen our friendship. Even after graduation, we continued to maintain a deep friendship by visiting each other in Japan and Korea. I came to feel that Japan, on a personal level, was a country with which I could establish a closer bond than with any other nation.

At the Halloween festival with children

The United States is entering the festive mood for the end of the year, starting with Halloween. Halloween is a tradition where people place candles inside hollowed-out pumpkins and set them in front of their houses. People dressed in white ghost costumes go door to door, handing out candy to children.

After the Halloween festival, Thanksgiving follows shortly after. Since the Thanksgiving holiday extends from the fourth Thursday of November, many people are excited and in a vacation mood. Following Thanksgiving come Christmas and New Year's, and amid the festive atmosphere, Americans are finding renewed energy in their lives. During the holiday period, many people meet with relatives and travel, visiting those who live far away and sharing conversations.

During this time, I also had the opportunity to travel. I was able to explore new places, not only within the United States, including Washington DC, Miami, Denver, and Las Vegas, but also abroad, traveling to Mexico, Canada, and other destinations. From November 4 to November 13, 1977, I traveled to Mexico with Major Noh Dong-jun and Colonel Sharif from Indonesia. The people of Mexico were very kind to us. We were able to visit historical sites, making the trip to Mexico a memorable experience. In particular, with the guidance of Colonel Heo Jung-il, the military attaché to Mexico, we were able to tour the country in detail.

I traveled to St. Louis, Atlanta, and the Orlando, Florida area during Christmas. Despite it being midwinter, I was able to swim at Miami Beach. I truly realized how vast the United States is, as in the summer, you can see snow in Alaska, and in the winter, you can swim in the sea in Miami. In Orlando, I visited Disney World and the John F. Kennedy Space Center, where I had the chance to witness the grandeur of America's space exploration efforts. Traveling through New Orleans, Houston, Dallas, and Oklahoma, I was once again able to confirm the immense strength and potential of the southern United States.

At Niagara Falls

In May 1978, I traveled through Washington DC, New York, and Canada. In Washington DC, I visited the Smithsonian, the

White House, and the U.S. Capitol. I was invited by General Park No-young, serving as a military attaché in the U.S., to receive a briefing on current issues regarding ROK/U.S. relations. I then moved north to see the magnificent Niagara Falls and traveled through Chicago and Pittsburgh, gaining a firsthand opportunity to understand American culture.

On the way back to Korea after completing my training, I took the opportunity to explore the remaining western United States. I visited the U.S. Air Force Academy in Colorado Springs. After the school tour, I explored nearby Native American historical sites, experiencing the Frontier spirit of the Western expansion era. After passing through Las Vegas, I arrived in Los Angeles, where I visited Hollywood and Universal Studios. Watching scenes from the Western movies I loved as a child, I felt as though I had returned to my childhood. During my travels, I was able to stay at Guest Houses on U.S. military bases, allowing me to travel across the United States at relatively low costs.

After returning to Korea, I gave a debriefing at a full generals' staff meeting attended by the Army Chief of Staff. When I explained a tactical plan that applied the new U.S. Army doctrines to fit the Korean environment, all the generals at the Army Headquarters applauded. After the meeting, the Army

Chief of Staff called me to his office. He instructed me to visit all the Korean military units and personally conduct explaining on the content I had reported. I enhanced the teaching with educational slides and, over the course of a month, traveled to corps-level units to teach the officers. The response across the entire military was overwhelming.

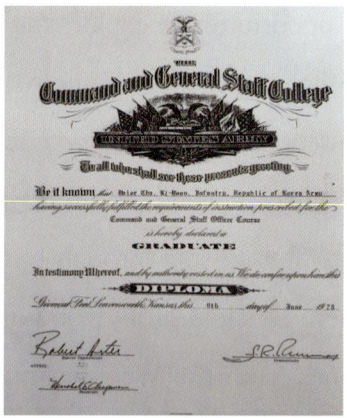

Graduating from the U.S. Army Command and General Staff College

I emphasized the concept that future warfare would no longer be fought along fixed front lines, but would instead require the maximum utilization of mobile reserve forces to be quickly deployed to danger zones. By introducing this new tactical concept to the entire military, my reputation spread widely. The new doctrine I presented was immediately reflected in the preparation of the operational plan 5027 for subordinate units, making a significant contribution to enhancing the defense capabilities of the Korean military.

4. Wargame Officer and Promotion to Lieutenant Colonel

After graduating from the U.S. Army Command and General Staff College, the position I was assigned to was at the ROK/US Combined Field Army Command, located in Uijeongbu. Normally, graduates of foreign command and general staff colleges are assigned as instructors at the Republic of Korea Army College in order to spread new doctrines. However, due to a strong request from the ROK/US Combined Field Army Command, I was assigned to the ROK/US Combined Field Army Command.

The ROK/US Combined Field Army Command was established after the end of the Vietnam War, when the 3rd Field Army Command was created. It was formed to execute operational control over the ROKA 1st, 5th, and 6th Corps, and the U.S. 2nd Infantry Division. The command was a joint force composed of both Korean and U.S. military personnel, with the U.S. handling facility management. Meals were served in a U.S. operated dining facility, and the Ministry of National Defense would settle the meal expenses for the Korean officers. Since I was eating Western food, I often found myself missing kimchi. Some people, after meals, would rush back to the BOQ and quickly take a bite of kimchi they had stored in the refrigerate.

Although the U.S. military held the position of commander, the staff members at the ROK/US Combined Field Army Command were predominantly Korean military personnel. At the ROK/US Combined Field Army Command, a scientific method was used to develop operational plans using the "First Battle" wargame model. First Battle wargame was a model developed by the U.S. Army Command and General Staff College.

After graduating from the U.S. Army Command and General Staff College, I was appointed the wargame director, tasked with complementing Operational Plan 5027 through wargaming and spreading wargame techniques to the Korean military. I gathered key commanders and staffs from across the army and demonstrated wargames that simulated real combat while disseminating the new doctrine to all Korean military units. The primary defense area for Korea was the western front. The

Kaesong-Munsan and the Cheorwon Line were expected to be the most threatening attack routes, as they were the primary targets during the Korean War, where North Korean forces launched major attacks. At the ROK/US Combined Field Army Command, I served as the lead officer in charge of preparing specific wargame-based defensive plans for these critical lines.

First Battle wargame in the ROK/US Combined Field Army Command

It was time to be promoted from major to lieutenant colonel. All the candidates for promotion were nervous. No matter how good their experience was, the key to promotion was having a good recommendation ranking from the unit, so the main focus of the fierce competition was on who would get the best ranking within the unit. Within the unit, the prevailing opinion was that

I should be the number one based on both my experience and work performance. However, the deputy commander, who was a senior major about to retire, gave the number one spot to his secretary. This was such an irrational decision that the personnel officer raised an objection and brought the issue to light. As the issue became known to many, Major General Chun Doo-hwan, who was the commander of the 1st Division at the time, and Colonel Park Jun-byeong, who was in charge of army promotion project, proposed a solution. They argued that Captain Cha Kimoon, who had elevated the Korean military doctrine to the level of advanced countries and had drafted the Korean defense plan with real-world relevance through war games, should not be excluded from the promotion.

Since this fact was known by the Army Chief of Staff and other generals, special points were given to the promotion review committee, allowing me to be included on the promotion list. In the end, both the secretary of the ROK/US Combined Field Army Command and I were promoted. When I later heard about this indirectly, I realized that the promotion system in our army was still alive and well. I came to believe that if one work according to one's convictions and faith, the result will be determined by God.

Later, General Kim Jae-myung was appointed as the new ROK/US Combined Field Army Command Korean side military commander. Since I had worked with him at the ROK/US Combined Planning Staff, he and I had a good rapport. He had a strong sense of patriotism and firmly believed that the Korean military should take the lead in the defense of Korea. Although I was a major and the principal officer responsible for drafting Operation Plan 5027, I took the lead in discussions with US senior officers to ensure that Korea's intentions were reflected in every aspect of the operational plan. This rumor spread throughout the Korean military, and with the support of many, we successfully implemented the forward defense concept to repel North Korean attacks north of the Han River as intended by the Korean military.

5. Airborne Training During Leave

After successfully completing the ROK/US Combined Field Army Command war games derector and the Chief of Operations Planning, I was assigned as a battalion commander. Fortunately, my successor, Lieutenant Colonel Kim Dong-shin (later became the Minister of National Defense), was assigned early as my replacement, so I had a one-month grace period before taking on the battalion commander role. In our generation, it was not easy to have the opportunity to undergo airborne training. As mentioned earlier, I volunteered to take airborne training when I was a second lieutenant. I went to the 1st Field Army Command in Wonju, passed the physical fitness test, and received orders to join the Special Warfare Command's airborne training. I was just waiting for the start date. But then I got the order to go Vietnam war, and I missed the opportunity to undergo airborne training.

I had always made up my mind that I would take airborne training whenever the opportunity arose, but such opportunities were hard to come by. After the Vietnam War, airborne training was only available to soldiers serving in the Special Warfare Units, and regular soldiers had no chance to join the airborne training school.

With the permission of General Kim Jae-myung, the deputy commander of the ROK/US Combined Field Army Command, I decided to take a leave of absence and undergo airborne training before assuming my role as battalion commander. I went to the Special Warfare Command training center in Geoyeodong, Seoul, and walked straight into the training center commander's office. At the time, I didn't even know who the training center commander was. The commander was Colonel Jo Nam-pung, graduated the 18th class of the Korea Military Academy. Although I had never seen him before, he had a kind and dignified appearance.

"Sir! I am on leave and would like to undergo airborne training. please allow me to take the training."

"Everyone tries to avoid the tough training, so how can a you take leave to undergo such a difficult training?"

"I have wanted to take the training for a long time, but I never had the opportunity, so I haven't been able to do airborne training. I believe the soldier must undergo airborne training, which is why I came here directly. Please give me the chance."

"Airborne training requires permission from the Army Headquarters, so go to Army Headquarters and get approval, and I will allow you to take the training."

I went to Army Headquarters and found the Operations and Training Department. When I met the officer in charge of training at Army Headquarters, he was Lieutenant Colonel Kim Hyung-seon (the 19th class of the KMA). Lieutenant Colonel Kim, who I had studied with at the Republic of Korea Army College, allowed me to undergo the training as a special case.

Since everyone was avoiding the tough airborne training, it seemed strange that a senior officer wanted to take it so late, but he processed the paperwork. However, since the timing didn't match, I couldn't be placed in the oficer's class, and he said I would be assigned with the enlisted soldiers who were sent to the Special Warfare Command, suggesting that I join the 192nd airborne training class with soldiers.

I entered the training alongside the strong new recruits selected from Nonsan Recruit Center, and endured four weeks of tough training. During the training period, I was tempted to quit several times. During landing training, my thighs were covered in bruises, and during the wind-blast training, my entire body was bruised. It was undoubtedly unreasonable to undergo such intense physical airborne training at my age, having already reached the rank of lieutenant colonel. Even though I was wearing my rank insignia, I lived with the soldiers, sharing the same barracks, and while running every day, I developed a deep sense of camaraderie with them.

The instructors made me repeat the training even more harshly. The logic was that the older you were, the more solid the basic ground training needed to be in order to prevent bones from breaking during the actual jump. Sweat soaked my entire body, and when I placed my mouth on the faucet during break time, water continuously flowed into my body. At the time, my classmate of KMA, Major Kim Myung-sae and my cousin, Captain Kim Jin-hwang (Korea Military Academy 28th class), were assigned to the airborne training school. Although they were junior to me, the instructors, who were noncommissioned officers, showed no mercy. Whenever Major Kim and Captain Kim came to visit me, that was the only time I had a break. I waited eagerly for those moments, as they felt like saviors to me. After three weeks of ground training, the fourth week arrived, and it was time for the parachute jump. June 1, 1979, the day of the jump at Misari Sand Dunes, had come.

The moment I made my first jump as the first jumper, I received the news that Cha Jeong-seok had been born into this world. According to the family tradition, when a son is born, the family name must include the generational character. Therefore, the name of the newborn had to be chosen according to the family's genealogy. In the Cha family, the generational character for my son was "Seok". To avoid duplicating names within the same generation, I asked the head family in Daegu to suggest a name, and they sent "Cha Jeong-seok". I liked it, so I named my son Jeong-seok. Even though I heard the news of my son's birth, I was still in training, so I couldn't even visit the maternity hospital and felt sorry for my wife. I could only express my gratitude over the phone, and then I returned to training. The joy of hearing about my son lifted my spirits, and my fatigue seemed to melt away as I felt energized, as if I were flying in the sky.

Completion of Airborne Training, Class 192

To receive the airborne wings, everyone had to successfully complete four parachute jumps. On the day of the third jump, it rained heavily. The Han River flooded the sand dunes, and the Misari jump training field was filled with muddy water. As a result, the jump had to be carried out at the backup training field, Namseongdae (which later became a golf course and is now part of Wirye New Town). Since I was the highest-ranking person among the trainees, I was the first to jump out of the airplane.

As I descended, a strong wind blew, and my parachute got caught in a large tree at the General Administrative School. I hung from the tree for a long time, and eventually, an instructor came over and cut the parachute lines with a knife, safely lowering me to the ground. This reminded me of the movie scenes where paratroopers in real combat fell into church crosses or pigpens. After completing the four jumps, I earned my airborne wings. During the training, I regretted joining the airborne training several times, but once it was over, I couldn't contain the joy, as if I were flying in the sky.

After the training was completed, I received orders to serve as a battalion commander. Initially, I was assigned as the commander of the infantry battalion of the 1st Division, but the orders were later revised, and I was appointed as the commander of the Reconnaissance Battalion of the 9th Division. Since I had completed airborne training alone, I was assigned to the position of commander of the newly established Reconnaissance Battalion of the 9th Division. At the time, the commander of the 1st Division was General Chun Doo-hwan (who later became the President of the Fifth Republic of Korea), and the commander of the 9th Division was General Roh Tae-woo (who later became the

President of the Sixth Republic of Korea). After consulting with each other, they issued the order for me to become the commander of the Reconnaissance Battalion of the 9th Division.

6. Commander of the 9th Division's Reconnaissance Battalion

On November 28, 1979, I was appointed as the commander of the Reconnaissance Battalion of the 9th Infantry Division. A grand battalion inauguration ceremony and my assumption of command took place at the battalion parade ground in Ilsan, under the supervision of Division Commander Roh Tae-woo. My classmates from Daeryun High School, as well as fellow officers from the Korea Military Academy, both seniors and juniors, attended in large numbers, and many family members, including my father-in-law, General Kim Seon-gyu, came to congratulate me.

The newly established Reconnaissance Battalion was set up in the fields of Ilsan, where buildings were constructed and soldiers were assigned from various units to form the battalion. The newly formed unit was not composed solely of new recruits but also included seasoned soldiers selected from each unit. This was because if the battalion were made up entirely of new recruits, not only would the soldiers be discharged at the same time, but the unit's combat capability would not be balanced. Therefore, soldiers of various ranks were selected from each unit to form the new battalion.

The establishment of the 9th Division Reconnaissance Battalion
(From left to right: General Roh Tae-woo, and The Author)

However, rather than sending their best soldiers, each unit sent only the most troublesome soldiers. As a result, the quality of the soldiers in our reconnaissance battalion was not very good. Additionally, the location chosen for building the battalion barracks was a graveyard, so when the ground was dug with an excavator, unclaimed bones were revealed. Once the building was completed and the soldiers started sleeping there, some of the weaker soldiers claimed to see ghosts under their beds and would run outside in fear.

The officers of the Reconn Battalion (I am standing third from the left.)

The training ground was an area that had been filled in, so whenever it rained, the ground would become extremely muddy. When spring came and the ground thawed, it became even more soggy for a longer period. I decided that the first priority was to improve the training ground, which was the soldiers' main courtyard. I installed drainage systems, brought in gravel, spread it across the training ground, and then covered it with sand. Only then did we have a proper training ground.

Amid these challenges, it was important to instill a sense of pride and confidence in the soldiers to transform the unit into one with the highest combat capability. A White Horse mark, featuring an axe as its background, was created and attached to their chests. Through distinctive and rigorous training as reconnaissance soldiers of the White Horse Division, the unity of the unit was fostered.

The company positions were as follows: the 1st Company was located at the Han River estuary's Breakthrough Line, the 2nd Company was stationed at Jeongbalsan, and the 3rd Company was positioned with the battalion. The embankment located at the Han River estuary was referred to as the Breakthrough Line. The battalion commander primarily spent time at the forward position of the 1st Company overseeing the counter infiltration operations from the Breakthrough Line. The 1st Company achieved significant results, such as eliminating armed enemy infiltrators during the rising tide.

There was only one road leading towards the Munsan area, which was Route 1. During tactical discussions, many suggested that constructing a highway along the Breakthrough Line at the Han River estuary would not only help with the defense of the area but also contribute significantly to traffic communication. Based on this suggestion, later, General Roh Tae-woo, who became president, oversaw the construction of the Freedom Road, which connected the Han River estuary to Panmunjom, alongside the development of the Ilsan New Town.

Through rigorous training and the spirit of unit camaraderie, which quickly took root, our unit was selected as the vanguard battalion of the corps just one year after its establishment. The unit received the following accolades: on June 20, 1980, it was recognized as the Best Battalion in Combat Readiness, on August 14, 1980, as the Best Unit in Combat Inspection, on September 20, 1980, as the Best Unit in Command, on October 21, 1980, as the Best Training Unit, and on November 20, 1980, as the Best Battalion in ATT. Finally, on December 28, 1980, our unit was honored with the distinction of being selected as the First Army Corps' vanguard battalion.

The achievements in developing the battalion into the best unit of the corps within just one year of its establishment were recognized, and a continuous stream of visits and morale-boosting measures followed. In this atmosphere, the battalion commander organized events such as ice skating competitions in the winter and sports competitions in the summer to boost the morale of the soldiers. As a result of efforts to improve physical fitness and morale, the battalion's soldiers won first place in various division and corps-level competitions, and their morale soared to great heights.

After winning the division competition
(I am in the center, wearing a leather jacket and sunglasses)

During the period when I served as the battalion commander, my son, Cha Jeong-seok, was a young child celebrating his first birthday. On holidays, the soldiers would take Cha Jeong-seok to the barracks and dining hall, feeding him military meals and playing with him. Growing up in this environment, Cha Jeong-seok became accustomed to military life and developed a fondness for the military by reading military-related books.

Every Sunday, the Division Chaplain, Shin Mun-gu would call. "Commander, you must come to church today." After sending a Bible following the welcome service for my appointment as Battalion Commander, he persistently called and visited, urging me to attend church.

My family and my wife's family had long followed Buddhism. During high school, I attended church to learn English from missionaries, and as a cadet at the Army Academy, I went to church to get snacks, but I had no religious faith. The division chaplain targeted us as a couple. Since it was a newly established unit, he viewed missionary work with the commander as a golden opportunity. Due to the persistent phone calls from Chaplain Shin Mun-gu every Sunday, my wife and I started attending church together. As the Bible says, "The last will be first," the late faith I began as a lieutenant colonel brought me closer to God.

While attending church, my wife became known among the battalion soldiers as a caring and kind mother. On cold nights, she would brew coffee and distribute it to the sentries, and after major training events, she would prepare rice cakes and fruit to share with the soldiers. Seeing this, Chaplain Assistant Shim Seung-jong would follow her around and assist her. After completing his service, Chaplain Assistant Shim became a pastor and went to the United States to engage in ministry, forming a deep and lasting bond with our family.

Lieutenant Jo Yong-deok, who served in the 3rd Company, asked me to officiate his wedding. At first, I was taken aback because it was the first time in my life at the age of 37 that I would be officiating a wedding. However, I couldn't refuse the request of a beloved subordinate, so I carefully prepared and delivered a heartfelt and meaningful ceremony. Because it was my first time officiating, I have maintained a deep and lasting relationship with Lieutenant Jo and his family, continuing to interact with them over the years.

7. The Military Faction Scandal

When I was active duty, there was a clandestine faction within the military called Hanahoe. From the 11th to the 36th class of the Korea Military Academy, around 10 elite officers from each class of KMA formed a group called Hanahoe. The officers who joined this organization addressed each other as older brother and younger brother, establishing strong personal relationships where they helped each other from above and pushed each other from behind.

Kyunghyang Shinmun, May 11, 1993

The roots of Hanahoe can be traced back to President Park Chung-hee. The elite officers from the 11th class of the Korea Military Academy came under President Park's special attention and protection, and it was around them that Hanahoe began to take shape. The individuals selected for this organization were typically officers who served in the Capital Security Command (later the Capital Defense Command) during their junior officer years. Since the officers from the Capital Security Command formed the core, the group was primarily composed of infantry, although 1~2 artillery officers were also included. As the Military Police had fewer opportunities for general officer promotions, only 1~2 officers from each KMA class were selected for Hanahoe, due to potential conflicts among peers after reaching the colonel rank.

The organization did not designate a general representative or chairman separately. Instead, it was managed by the most senior members or those in key positions who could exert substantial influence within the military, such as the Commander of the Security Command. These individuals formed the core, with intermediate bosses placed at appropriate intervals to manage the organization. The membership was structured into two categories: the core group, referred to as the "sungol", consisting of 3~4 key members, and the "jingol", who were considered peripheral members. The core group was continuously assigned to positions within the capital region for frequent exchanges of opinions, while the others were often assigned to more remote posts.

Funds were necessary to operate the organization, and

Hanahoe did not collect membership dues or contributions for events and celebrations. Instead, it operated by attracting sponsors during social gatherings. The core group, which was composed of key members, maintained a discreet hierarchical relationship, and interactions occurred among all members, from the senior veterans to the junior officers of the 36th class. However, the non-core members, who had significant differences in class years, often did not know each other unless there was a special matter that required contact.

Promotions and assignments were managed by the core group, which held control over personnel decisions. This was done through positions like Director of the Personnel Department, Director of Personnel Management, Personnel Control Officer, Promotion Officer, General Personnel Officer at the Army Headquarters, as well as personnel officers of the Third Army Command. These positions were filled with junior members of Hanahoe, who then managed personnel matters for their fellow members. As a result of this system, all members up to the 29th class received their first promotion to colonel.

Members of Hanahoe who lacked character and qualities sometimes had a tendency to look down on other senior members. While they would show great respect to Hanahoe seniors, they would display a disrespectful attitude toward those who were not Hanahoe members. In some cases, non-Hanahoe seniors found Hanahoe juniors to be a burden.[3]

The exclusive personnel practices of Hanahoe led to the monopolization of key positions and promotions, causing them to unite only among themselves, which hindered overall military cohesion and created a sense of division. As a result, public opinion began to spread regarding the negative side effects of this situation. After the Kim Young-sam government took power, it sharpened its efforts to dismantle military clandestine factions. First, since Hanahoe was a secretive organization, its existence did not officially come to light.

On April 2, 1993, the "Hanahoe list distribution" incident occurred at the Dongbinggo Military Apartment in Seoul, which led to an official investigation.

The investigation gained momentum when Colonel Baek Seung-do, the individual responsible for distributing the Hanahoe list, voluntarily reported to the Army Headquarters Military Police Office on April 16, 1993. The Hanahoe Fact-Finding Committee

---

[3] Jo Wang-ho, Modern Korean History for Youth, Duri Media, 2006, pp. 129-135.

was formed, chaired by the Deputy Chief of Staff of the Army Headquarters, and included six military legal officers. Due to legal limitations, the investigation was confined to active-duty personnel, and it was difficult to interview retired generals, which made it challenging to investigate the initial formation of the group.

Purge of Hanahoe by President Kim Young-sam

However, through a comprehensive investigative process, the civilian government confirmed the existence of Hanahoe and, as part of an effort to establish military control, carried out a large-scale personnel reshuffle. This ultimately led to the complete dismantling of the Hanahoe organization.

Hanahoe members were undoubtedly an excellent group of officers. However, the notion that those who were not part of Hanahoe were not excellent officers is incorrect. Among the non-Hanahoe officers, some were superior to the Hanahoe officers. These individuals had to put in much effort and possess the perseverance of bone-cutting determination and unyielding will.

I did not have the opportunity to serve at the Capital Security Command, so I was distanced from Hanahoe. For me, a non-Hanahoe member, rising to the rank of general in the first round was not easy. It was due to my top performance at various advanced training programs, including OAC, Republic of Korea Army College, and U.S. Army Command and General Staff College, as well as consistently receiving high evaluations across all ranks, and most importantly, God's grace.

8. Designated to the Samcheong Education Center

With the establishment of the Fifth Republic, the Samcheong Education was implemented under the pretext of social reform, with the aim of rehabilitating organized criminals and vagrants.

Our battalion also received orders to carry out the Samcheong Education. Barbed wire was installed at the unit, and equipment for the education, such as tents, dishes, and mattresses, was gradually supplied.

Due to the nature of the military, subordinate units must follow the orders of higher authorities. If they disobey such orders, it would constitute an act of insubordination. As the battalion commander, I am not in a position to judge whether this system is right or wrong. I have no choice but to follow the orders from above without question.

A proclamation from the Martial Law Commander was issued for the purpose of Samcheong Education. Following the proclamation, a total of 60,755 people were arrested nationwide by January 1981. They were classified into four categories—A, B, C, and D—by an evaluation committee consisting of the National Security Command, the Central Intelligence Agency, the Military Police, the Prosecutor's Office, the Police, and the Local Cleanup Committee. Category A included leaders of organized crime groups, habitual offenders of violence, armed robbers, and those caught in drug-related crimes. Category B consisted of members of organized crime groups, habitual gamblers, robbers, and smugglers. Category C included those with minor offenses or those who had committed less serious violence, as well as individuals in Category B who had their circumstances taken into account. Category D included first-time offenders, those with minor offenses, normal students and youths, and individuals with stable jobs and addresses who showed clear potential for improvement.

A-level 3,252 individuals were referred to military courts. B and C-level 39,786 individuals underwent four weeks of education, followed by six months of imprisonment, after which they received two weeks of education for corrective guidance. D-level 17,717 individuals were given corrective guidance by the police. Those classified as B and C-level were transferred to 26 units, under the surveillance of armed military and police personnel at police stations.[4] At that time, the B and C-level individuals assigned to the 9th Division were given corrective education by our reconnaissance battalion.

After the individuals entered the unit, they were given a bath and changed into training uniforms. Most of them had tattoos on their bodies, including snakes, naked women, weapons, and

---

4   Seo Young-su, *Samcheong Re-education Camp* (Seoul: HiBooks, 2004), pp. 98-105.

various other designs that gave off an unpleasant impression. Some individuals had undergone male genital modification, attaching strange objects. However, among them were also people who had been unfairly enrolled while leaving behind their beloved families. Despite the strict regulations, they were treated with humanity. I personally conducted interviews with each individual and sent home letters to assure their families not to worry. Through spiritual purification by the chaplains, priests, and military clerics, many people turned to religion. Those who showed good progress in their education were allowed special visits. Among the visitors were famous celebrities, movie stars, comedians, and politicians, which demonstrated the significant social influence they had.

Samcheong Education Camp

Incidents also occurred in other units during Samcheong education process. The enforcement of harsh training methods involving physical pain led to 54 deaths being reported during the 1988 National Defense Ministry audit. Among the individuals handed over by the police for re-education, some were wrongfully included. There were also cases where individuals were arrested due to accusations, some of which were linked to personal grievances.

The evaluation of the Samcheong education Camp will be made by future historians, but it can be said that both positive and negative aspects exist. While the purpose of its establishment at the time was good, there were individuals who were unjustly and irrationally included during the selection process, which should be criticized. In particular, if there were cases of suppressing democratic forces and human rights violations, such unreasonable history should never be repeated.

After undergoing the establishment of the reconnaissance battalion and the 12.12 Military Insurrection, I took charge of the Samcheong Re-education Camp and completed my term as the battalion commander amidst the turbulent waves of history. After finishing my term as the battalion commander, I served in the Joint Chiefs of Staff and later attended the National

Defense University. After graduating from the National Defense University, I successfully served as the Director of Combat Division 1 at the Personnel Management Office of Army Headquarters and then became a Regiment Commander.

9. The Best Regiment in the RCT

On May 30, 1985!

I assumed the position of the Commander of the 76th Regiment, 26th Division. Located in Deokjeong, Yangju-gun, Gyeonggi Province, the regiment was known as one of the most traditional and outstanding units in the entire military. Upon entering the regimental commander's office, I noticed that all the past commanders' photos had stars marked on them. This signified that all past commanders of the 76th Regiment had become generals.

General Lee Byeong-tae, the 26th Division Commander, (the 17th class of the Korea Military Academy, later the Minister of National Defense), was a highly respected leader in the military. He was known for his excellent command of strong character, and virtue, earning the admiration of his juniors. The division commander gave a grand ceremony for the regimental commander's inauguration. Among the 23rd class of the Korea Military Academy, I, who had always been promoted in the first round and possessed exceptional qualities in tactics and strategy, was highly anticipated. In the neighboring 73rd and 75th Regiments, senior officers, Colonel Lee Yeon-woo and Colonel Heo Jang-do (the 22nd class of KMA), were assigned to their respective positions.

Inauguration ceremony of the 76th Regiment Commander

Once assigned as the regimental commander, it is mandatory to conduct a Regimental Combat Team (RCT) exercise at least once during the tenure. Our 76th Regiment conducted the RCT training in the Han River region, engaging in a bilateral exercise with the 36th Regiment of the 5th Division. To raise the morale for the RCT training, I hung banners in the barracks, dining halls, and other areas where soldiers gathered to inspire a fighting spirit. I also had the soldiers wear ribbons on their chests to instill a sense of pride in participating in the training, and through free discussions, each soldier was made to recognize the importance of the exercise.

On the way to the decisive battlefield of the RCT

The focus was placed on clearly defining the training objectives for the unit, ensuring that the regiment would operate in accordance with the regimental commander's intentions. The outcome of the battle depends on how effectively the attached support units are controlled and integrated into the parent unit, the regiment. I believed that utilizing superior army aviation assets to target the enemy's weaknesses would be the key to victory.

The Fire Eagle demonstration

By coincidence, the corps issued a directive for our regiment to demonstrate Fire Eagle, an integrated operation between aviation and infantry units. This was a great opportunity to apply it to the RCT training. Fire Eagle is an army firepower integration close combat that combines all ground force firepower means, including aviation, artillery, tanks, Tow, and 106mm recoilless rifles. It is a tactical operation that forms an aerial fire support team to integrate attack helicopters, howitzers, and ground antitank weapons, enabling a rapid and timely response to enemy mechanized and armored units that appear in the close combat area.

Emphasis was placed on perfect operational security. Fighting without knowing the enemy is like a boxer stepping into the ring with his eyes closed. Since the enemy will do their best to gather intelligence on our forces, it is extremely important to protect our operational capabilities from enemy surveillance. The frequency of changing the Communication Electronics Operating Instructions (CEOI) was changed from every four days to every day. We used code designations and checkpoints to ensure that no communication was conducted in plain text. We also made the use of field-grade direction-finding antennas mandatory on all radios.

Preparations for preventing safety accidents were essential for drivers handling maneuver equipment over long distances and in unfamiliar terrain. Since most of the marches took place at night, measures to prevent drivers from falling asleep were a major concern. To keep them awake, non-drowsy medication was provided to the drivers, along with chewing gum and candy. During the day, an environment conducive to rest was created so that they could get sufficient sleep when not on duty. Our regiment, having thoroughly prepared for the RCT, moved to the Hantan River and entered the exercise as if it were actual combat. Corps Commanding General Park Myeong-cheol, accompanied by Operations Officer Colonel Yeo Myeong-hyeon (21st class of KMA) and other staff officers, personally oversaw and directed the training on-site for five nights and six days. Positioned across the Hantan River, the regiment had to establish an operational plan based on intelligence it obtained on its own capabilities. The intelligence provided by higher commands was extremely limited.

Corps CDR Park Myeong-cheol is listening to briefing after an unannounced visit.

Corps Commander Park Myeong-cheol made unannounced visits to the regimental command post to assess how the regimental commander was handling the situation. During the tense five-night, six-day period, it was impossible to get even an hour of proper sleep each day. With a firm conviction to win, a decision was made to deceive the enemy, direct the main attack toward the area with the weakest enemy deployment, and then encircle and annihilate the enemy.

Deceptive signs were deliberately exposed to the enemy to suggest a crossing operation downstream of the Hantan River. Once this false intelligence reached the enemy, the opposing 35th Regiment commander concentrated his main forces in the downstream area. Seizing this opportunity, our regiment moved its main force upstream, successfully crossed the river, and cut off the enemy's retreat. With the enemy completely encircled, we achieved a major victory.

The regimental commander took the lead and personally crossed the Hantan River, fully clothed, with the water reaching up to his waist. As it was winter, the lower body felt as if it were completely frozen. The riverbed was slippery, and even the slightest loss of balance could result in falling into the water—a dangerous situation. However, when the regimental commander entered the water himself, the staff officers and battalion commanders followed him, and then all the soldiers entered the river as well, successfully crossing without a single straggler. The surprise attack exploiting the enemy's vulnerability was fully achieved. Once the surprise attack succeeded, the enemy could be guided according to our intentions. Caught off guard by the sudden assault, the enemy lost cohesion and fell into disarray, and the battle concluded with a one-sided victory for our regiment.

Witnessing the scene firsthand, Corps Commander Park Myeong-cheol praised our 76th Regiment during the debriefing, declaring it on the spot as the best-performing regiment among all those under the corps' command in the RCT training. Through this experience, it became clear that the firm belief in inevitable victory and the commander's example of taking the lead in front of the troops are the very essence of leadership and command.

After returning victorious from the RCT, the regiment held an after-action review meeting and then ensured ample rest during the maintenance period. The previously postponed leaves, outings, and overnight passes were boldly granted. What soldiers appreciate most is, above all, vacation and outings. Reward leave was granted generously, focusing on the soldiers who had made significant contributions during the RCT training.

Review meeting after the RCT exercise

The morale of not only the soldiers but also the officers was important. Since the Lunar New Year was approaching, traditional holiday games, including yutnori, were organized for the officers. All officers' gatherings were held with their spouses to help foster a wholesome family culture.

10. Vanguard Regiment in the Team Spirit Exercise

Just as the unit maintenance was nearing completion following the RCT, the phone in the regimental commander's office rang loudly. It was Division Commander Lee Byeong-tae calling to inform me that our 76th Regiment would be participating in the Team Spirit '86 exercise. What thrilling news I had been waiting for! Being selected to take part in Team Spirit, the largest exercise in the world, was an honor not only for the unit but also for the regimental commander, and I couldn't calm my excitement for some time after receiving the call.

Since my regiment had successfully completed the RCT, it was the shared desire of all troops to carry that momentum into the globally renowned Team Spirit exercise. Moreover, since the entire division would be participating, it was a golden opportunity to demonstrate to the public our full combat potential—enough to go to war tomorrow and win. Team Spirit was the world's largest maneuver exercise, where U.S. Army, Navy, Air Force, and Marine Corps units stationed in the continental U.S. and overseas bases were deployed to the Korean Peninsula to conduct combined operations with the ROK forces.

The focus of my training was on boosting the morale of all unit personnel to promote unity and trust within the regiment. The goal was to fully integrate the support units, which were usually separated, so that all elements of combined arms operations could be completely mastered. By ensuring perfect operational security, we prevented any intelligence leaks, no matter how hard the enemy tried to assess our situation. Emphasis was also placed on maintaining discipline to avoid any loss of combat power due to safety accidents, and on preventing any damage to civilians. These training priorities and guidelines were conveyed to Major Kim Hyeon-woo, the regimental operations officer, to ensure thorough preparation for the joint exercise.

Arrival at the operation area welcomed by local residents

After a three-month preparation period, the unit began its movement to the Chungju area, located along the Namhan River. We referred to this operation as the "Battle of Chungju." The long-distance march from my unit to Chungju encountered many challenges.

The issue was that the unit had to move along Route 3, which had heavy traffic, without traffic control. Military police were stationed at each intersection, and by using the late-night hours, we were able to successfully move 100 vehicles while conducting fuel resupply. Heavy Equipment, which were normally used in wartime, were moved to the operation area via rail. As the vanguard of the division, the regiment was tasked with crossing the Namhan River and seizing the Bakdaljae pass. The river crossing operation was no easy task. After conducting a thorough reconnaissance of the crossing points with the staff, the operation was carried out.

The regiment's staff conducted a reconnaissance of the Namhan River crossing area(I am standing third from the left.)

In the "Battle of Chungju," the regiment focused on thoroughly assessing the enemy with the concept of "fighting with the enemy in the palm of my hand." During delay operations, the reconnaissance platoon was left behind in the enemy's territory to maintain surveillance on key positions. A separate enemy radio interception team was organized in the regiment's operations room to listen in on enemy communications. It only took 20 minutes for our regiment's signal soldiers to identify the enemy's frequency.

The lesson that "attack is the best form of defense" is a common truth in combat. Defense is merely a part of the attack. In battle, there is only attack, and all other forms of combat are just auxiliary means to support the attack. All operations were designed to ensure the application of an offensive concept in the deployment of forces. Therefore, even during the defense phase, our regiment focused on breaking attacks, counterattacks, and small unit offensive operations, which led to significant success in fighting the enemy. The goal of a breaking attack was to disrupt the enemy's balance before they could form their attacking formation.

Having seized the intermediate objective during the attack, our regiment assigned a tank company to Colonel Kim Chang-su, the commander of the 3rd Battalion, as a reserve unit, directing them to bypass Guksabong and attack. Another tank platoon from the regiment's reserves was tasked with attacking Mun-nam 30 minutes before the attack commenced, carrying out a pincer maneuver. As the attack progressed, it appeared the enemy was having their evening meal, and when Colonel Kim's battalion, led by tanks, launched the attack, the enemy soldiers were thrown into disarray.

The enemy battalion commander, in desperation, abandoned trucks on the road as obstacles and fled. However, the trucks were nothing more than paper scraps in front of the tanks. With the speed of the attack, the enemy tanks, which were gathered in the rear, hadn't even started their engines yet. By combining the Fire Eagle tactics used in the RCT with the attack, the effectiveness was greatly amplified.

Since the enemy's main force was positioned around Highway 38, Pyeongdong became the enemy's only escape route. Cheondung Mountain, mentioned in the song "The Parkdaljae That One Sobs to Overcome," was a typical terrain that could encircle the enemy's main forces. It was judged that if my regiment seized Pyeongdong early, the operation, which would normally take two days, could be concluded in half a day.

After winning the Battle of Chungju
(From the front row, left to right: Personnel Officer Major Oh Jun-seop, The Author)

Using the treacherous mountain paths, a battalion-level infiltration maneuver was carried out while advancing. After blocking the targets in the enemy's rear, a combined operation of infantry, armor, and artillery pressed the surrounded enemy, making their annihilation an easy task. After blocking Pyeongdong and psychologically paralyzing the retreating enemy, a disruption operation was conducted from the mountain using gongs, jingles, drums, and trumpet sounds. The enemy fell into a state of panic, and the morale of our soldiers soared to the sky. Through this battle, it was confirmed that infiltration encirclement maneuvers are more effective than direct assaults or breakthroughs.

The Team Spirit joint exercise was an extremely valuable training. In particular, the combined operation with the 2nd Infantry Division of the United States helped greatly in resolving and understanding obstacles such as language and doctrinal issues. Conducting large-scale exercises at the corps level or higher with a US/ROK Combined force is not only meaningful in itself, but such exercises are also a key measure and essential strategy for deterring war in advance.

However, in the context of the progress in inter-Korean relations following the 1991 South-North Basic Agreement, the CFC side decided to suspend the Team Spirit exercise scheduled for 1992. Later, as inter-Korean relations deteriorated due to the North Korean nuclear issue, the CFC sides decided to resume the exercise in October 1992. It conducted a scaled-down version of the exercise in 1993. However, following the 1994 DPRK-U.S. Geneva Agreement, the Team Spirit joint exercise was completely halted.

11. Selected as the Operations Officer of the 6ᵗʰ Corps

It is customary to appoint a colonel with bright future prospects, who has successfully completed the mission of a regiment commander, as the corps operations officer. This is because the corps operations officer position almost guarantees promotion to general, making it a coveted role that everyone aspires to. The corps commander also wants to assign the most competent officer to the most important position.

On a day in December 1986, General Lee Byung-tae, the division commander, informed me that I had been selected as the operations officer for the 6ᵗʰ Corps. At that time, General Na Byeong-seon (14ᵗʰ class of KMA), the commander of the 6ᵗʰ Corps, was someone I had neither worked with nor had the opportunity to get close to. The fact that General Na, whom I did not know well, appointed me as his key staff member was due to the advice from many people that I needed to become the operations officer for the development of the corps. The former operations officer, Colonel Ye Myeong-hyun (21ˢᵗ class of KMA), was known as an outstanding officer among his peers and successfully completed his duties as the operations officer, earning a promotion to general before transferring to another assignment.

The Commander of the ROK/US CFC, General Lipsy, and The Author

The 6th Corps was a key unit on the western front, responsible for the approach routes to Jeonggok. Since it operated under the operational control of the ROK/US Combined Field Army Command, the operations officer had to be proficient in English. The corps frequently conducted joint operations with U.S. forces, and it often took part in the Team Spirit exercise, where it was a leading unit, controlling U.S. 2nd Infantry Division and other subordinate units. Given these responsibilities, the 6th Corps needed an operations officer who could speak English, and since I had previously served as the operations officer at the ROK/US Combined Field Army Command, I was considered the most suitable candidate for the position of the corps operations officer.

At the age of 43, I was appointed as the operations officer of the 6th Corps, and I devoted all my efforts to the development of the corps, based on the experiences and education I had accumulated. The 40s are the most productive period of life. It is a time when one can stay up for days without worrying about health, and mentally perform at the highest level. As the corps' operations officer, I was able to fully unleash my potential, and in terms of productivity, this period was the golden age of my life.

While carrying out my duties as the Corps G3, General Na Byeong-seon, the corps commander, left, and General Lim In-jo (the 17th class of KMA), took over as the new corps commander. After I inspect the front-line areas with General Lim In-jo, we encountered severe weather on our way back. During this time, the helicopter carrying us lost its direction in mid-air. Suddenly, a snowstorm began to blow, obscuring the visibility, and the helicopter was no longer able to fly. As the night grew darker, the helicopter tilted left and right in the strong winds, and we couldn't regain control of its direction. I thought to myself, "This is how it ends." When a helicopter crashes, it usually falls to the ground like scrap metal, and most of the time, it results in death.

Front-line GP inspection (I am standing on the left in the front row.)

However, the skilled pilot managed to overcome this crisis. Although the tail wing of the helicopter struck a tree, it tilted and made an emergency landing in the wilderness. If we hadn't been wearing seatbelts, we would all have been on our way to the afterlife. As night fell and everything turned pitch black, we were safely rescued by the soldiers from a nearby unit who came after receiving the distress call.

One of the most difficult issues while serving in the field was the education of my children. My daughter Cha Soo-jin was attending school at her maternal grandparents' house. We had become a separated family. My father-in-law and mother-in-law, who had already married off all their children, treated Cha Soo-jin as their own daughter and took very good care of her. Cha Soo-jin grew up well, thinking of her maternal grandparents as her parents, and she followed them closely. She was also very bright and did well in her studies.

My son, Cha Jeong-seok, is on the far right with his friends

My son, Cha Jeong-seok, was still young and attending elementary school in Pocheon, where the corps was stationed. Cha Jeong-seok adapted well to the new environment, making friends and attending Pocheon Elementary School. One day, mischievous Cha Jeong-seok and his friends set fire to the grass in the corps' quarters, and when the wind picked up, the fire spread, turning the quarters into a sea of flames. Eventually, the fire was carried by the wind to the Corps commander's residence. Fire trucks were dispatched, and all military personnel were mobilized, but Cha Jeong-seok, undaunted, took the lead in putting out the fire.

"Put it out here!"

"There's fire over there too!"

People couldn't help but laugh, even though they were upset. Fortunately, the fire was extinguished by the fire truck before it reached the Corps commander's residence. General Im In-jo, the corps commander, would often pat Cha Jeong-seok's head and recount that moment whenever he saw him.

Meeting the President Roh Tae-woo just before the 1988 Olympic Games

During the two years I served as the corps G3, my weight dropped to 50 kg. It was a time when more focus had to be placed on combat readiness, especially with the 1988 Olympics approaching. The KAL plane bombing incident occurred, and armed North Korean terrorists frequently appeared in the rear area. People were concerned about the security risks of hosting the Olympics in a divided country where full peace had not yet been established.

The operations room always had a field bed prepared. There were more nights spent in the office than at home. Meals were taken with boxed lunches, and since I had to think a lot, I smoked a lot of cigarettes. This was when I smoked the most in my life. However, even under these difficult conditions, I felt that nothing was impossible for me, and I was confident about anything I set out to do.

There was a sense of reward for working hard as I made it to the list of brigadier general promotions in the first round among the 23rd class of the Korea Military Academy. I was so absorbed in my work that I didn't have the time to focus on the promotion evaluation. However, with my unparalleled experience, evaluation, educational performance, and current position, I was able to make it onto the list of top group general candidates.

Chapter 3

•

| The Years as a General |

1. Chief of Staff of the 5th Corps

January 1, 1989!

I was promoted to the general. Over the course of 22 years since my commissioning, there were many ups and downs, but at the age of 45, I became the first among my classmates to be promoted to general. After the promotion, I handed over the position of 6th Corps G3 to Colonel Kim Pan-gyu (24th class of KMA), who was serving as the personnel officer of the 6th Corps, and was promoted to Chief of Staff of the 5th Corps. When I was serving as the 6 corps G3, I smoked a lot, but I quit smoking upon my promotion to general.

The formal announcement of my promotion began with a visit to the National Cemetery. It was a moment to express my gratitude to the fallen heroes who devoted their lives for the country and the people, and a vow to dedicate this life to the country and the nation. The ceremony for the promotion to general was held in a grand manner. While the artillery salute for the general rank was fired, I received the salute from the troops and pinned the silver stars on both shoulders.

Ceremony for promotion to a general

When promoted to the rank of general, many things change. The president presents the "Samjeongdo". It is a sword that the general owns for the rest of their life, symbolizing the heavy responsibility entrusted to them for the country and the people. Starting from the rank of general, the distinction of branches of service disappears, and the term "general" signifies that a general is proficient in all fields.

Generals are given a nameplate and a general's flag. The

army's nameplate and flag have a red background, the navy's have a dark navy blue background, and the air force's have a blue background with silver stars shining. The nameplate is always attached to the vehicle to indicate that the general is in the car. The general's flag, with a large star embroidered on a golden-threaded flag, is hoisted wherever the general goes. Wearing distinctive general's shoes with zippers, a general's jacket, a general's hat, and a general's uniform made me feel the heavy responsibility of being a general.

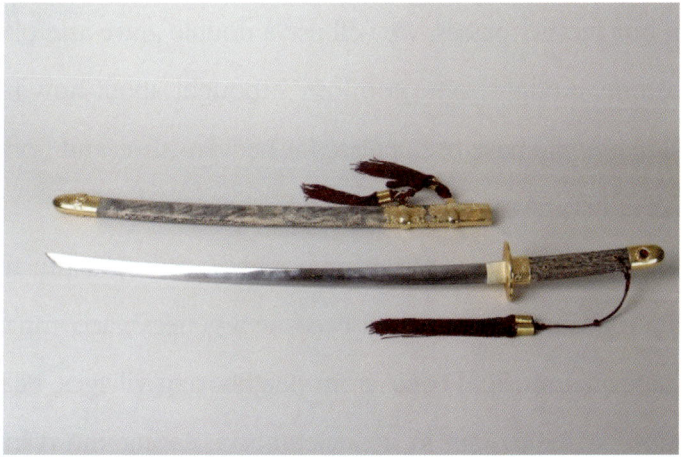

Samjeongdo

An aide-de-camp and a driver were assigned. The aide-de-camp accompanies the general 24 hours a day, providing personal assistance. The saying that generals, right after retirement, don't know how to make a phone call, don't know the way, and don't know how to drive comes from the aide-de-camp handling all the general's personal affairs.

I visited my hometown after a long time. Being tied up with my busy military duties, I had been an unfilial child who couldn't even tidy up my ancestors' graves, but I went to visit my father's grave to greet him after my promotion to general. When I went to the grave in my hometown, Bammgol, with my brothers, a shabby grave of my father awaited, and I couldn't help but feel a deep sense of sadness. The words of my eldest brother, that when our mother passes, we will use a double grave and place a tombstone, brought some comfort. I thought about how much my father would have been pleased if he were alive, and I offered a drink at his grave.

The people of my hometown were holding a big feast, celebrating the fact that I had become a general, accompanied by traditional music. People from neighboring villages, hearing the news, came to join in the celebration, eating and drinking without realizing how late it had gotten, filled with joy. Watching the passionate welcome from the hometown people for my promotion to general, I was reminded once again that I had come this far thanks to the kindness and consideration of those around me.

I paid my respects for my promotion at my father Cha Kyeung-bong's grave.
(From left to right: Cha Ki-whan, the author,
Cha Ki-hong, Cha Jeong-seok, Cha Won-seok)

I didn't have much time. I hurriedly finished greeting the elders in my family and headed to my assigned post at the 5th Corps Headquarters in Pocheon. General Jeong Man-gil (The 16th class of KMA), whom I didn't personally know well, became a member of the promotion evaluation committee. After assessing my abilities, he requested me to serve as the 5th Corps Chief of Staff. General Jeong, a key figure of the new military regime during the 5th Republic, had served in the National Security Planning Agency, and his demands could not be refused even by the Army Headquarters.

The 5th Corps is the main force of the South Korean military, responsible for the Iron Triangle area on the central front. It commands the 3rd, 6th, 8th, 66th, 73rd, and 75th divisions and operates under the operational control of the ROK/US Combined Field Army Command. General Jeong Man-gil, the corps commander, was widely known as a brilliant strategist and a capable general with meticulous planning skills and energetic drive.

The Chief of Staff is the overall commander responsible for the practical operations of the corps, overseeing the detailed management of the unit and checking and implementing combat situations. Upon taking office, I immediately began to familiarize myself with the duties of each staff and subordinate units. Since there were many units, it took considerable time to receive the initial reports on all of them. Day and night, I focused on understanding the operational situation and confirming the status of the units.

The corps is a formation that carries out assigned combat missions by organizing units, so the role of the direct-support units to the Corps is extremely important. Key combat support elements, such as artillery, special forces, engineers, communications, and chemical units, are organized under the corps' direct command. While the division operates as an independent unit with the division commander playing a central role, the corps' combat support units are commanded by the Chief of Staff.

At the inspection for combat readiness

I broke the tradition of sitting in my office with a pen and paper as the Chief of Staff, and instead, I visited the subordinate units directly to check their combat readiness. I personally confirmed whether the intentions of the corps command had been properly communicated to the subordinate units and whether we would be able to win if a war broke out that night. The war operations room was reorganized into an efficient and practical system that integrated mobility and firepower. I structured the system into a space and organization that allowed for clear and concise war mapping.

On May 26, 1989, General Jeong Man-gil left, and General Kim Dong-jin (The 17th Class of KMA) was appointed as the new corps commander. General Kim, who graduated first in his class from the Korea Military Academy and studied English literature at Seoul National University, was a commander with both wisdom and bravery, excelling in strategy and tactics. Later, he demonstrated outstanding leadership as the Chief of Staff of the Army and the Minister of National Defense, becoming a renowned general.

At Seungjin Firing Range, a demonstration of the largest ever spearhead annihilation operation, integrating mobility and firepower, was conducted. Centered around the 1st Armored Brigade, the operation involved air force fighter jets and special forces, resembling a real combat situation. The demonstration was attended by over 6,000 people, including the president, key government officials, general citizens, foreign military attachés, and defense industry representatives. Amidst a barrage of fire, the 1st Armored Brigade pierced through enemy fire and charged into enemy territory to capture the final objective in a maneuver operation.

The main figures of the spearhead annihilation operation and the Author (back row, from left to right: Yoo Jong-dae, Heo Seong, Lee Seong-gyu, Lee Si-chang)

Pocheon, where the corps headquarters is located, is known for its high mountains and deep valleys, making it a popular resort area. Due to its excellent water, the local Makgeolli (rice wine) was highly popular nationwide. A resort for soldiers was established in the deep valley of Gukmangbong. After completing training that resembled real combat, soldiers would check into the resort to rest and prepare for the next day's battle. During off-seasons without soldier relaxation, military families were also allowed to use the facilities as a considerate gesture.

It was an unprecedented large-scale operation that showcased the pinnacle of combined arms operations, integrating various branches of the military and joint operations between the Air Force and the Army. This operation, carried out with numerous troops firing live ammunition, carried significant concerns about safety accidents. Due to a major incident in the past, extra precautions were taken to ensure safety, allowing the operation to be completed successfully.

After successfully completing a one-year term as the 5th Corps Chief of Staff, I was assigned to the position of Personnel Officer at the 2nd Operational Command, marking my first time serving in a rear-area post during my military career. From my commissioning as a second lieutenant to becoming a general, I had only served in frontline areas, and after a long time, I was assigned to serve in Daegu, where my hometown is located.

2. Serving at Coast Guard Posts on the East, West, and South Coasts

The 2nd Operational Command was my first experience working in a rear-area unit during my military service, and there were many unfamiliar aspects. The area was coastal, and the operational region was vast, so it differed significantly from frontline duty. The terrain was new, the unit structure differed from that of frontline units, and even the terminology used in performing tasks was unfamiliar. There were times when I couldn't understand the documents brought by the junior officers for approval. I even had difficulty understanding the content presented at various meetings. Under these circumstances, I couldn't continue my service at the 2nd Operational Command. So I decided to go out to the subordinate units and experience the field firsthand to better understand the work. I first visited the battalion-level command post to assess the situation, then began walking along the coastline, starting from Uljin and following the East, South Coast, and eventually to the West Coast at Dangjin. It was often midnight when I arrived at the posts and sub-posts. We would have instant noodles as a late-night snack during the overnight shift change between the front and rear duty teams. The taste of eating noodles after standing guard all night was more satisfying than the finest royal banquet. When I asked the soldiers what their favorite snack was, they all answered, "Ramen." I understood why this was the case. This experience taught me that the soldiers' favorite snack was not fancy bread or fruit, but instant noodles.

Following the coastal guard post patrol route, there were times I got caught in the rain. At times, the weather was so harsh that sand blown by the wind made it nearly impossible to see ahead. Platoon leaders recommended I take a short rest at their posts. However, bound by a tight schedule to inspect the entire coastline, I pushed on without resting, marching until the soles of my feet were blistered, and finally reached the final destination, the Dangjin post.

Serving on coastal guard posts

During the inspection, there was an incident where a radar base mistakenly issued an alert for an enemy infiltration. While standing guard on a barge with the soldiers, we had a mishap in which a fishing boat was mistaken for a spy vessel. The sense of accomplishment from having personally inspected the entire coastline on foot completely washed away all the fatigue I had felt. I was filled with confidence that I knew more about the operational status of the 2nd Operational Command area than anyone else. It goes without saying that this invaluable experience was of tremendous help to my military career. When I was first assigned, I was like a chick when it came to coastal operations, but later I was able to engage in the most dynamic discussions during various meetings and briefings. The insights I gained through firsthand experience came to be recognized as the most authoritative opinions. As with everything, but especially in military affairs, I was reminded once again that on-site experience is the most precious and valuable asset.

Because the 2nd Operational Command was located in the large city of Daegu, there were frequent interactions with civilians. Rear area operations can only succeed with the absolute support of local residents. The military is like a fish, and the people are like water. Just as a fish cannot survive without water, military operations cannot succeed without the cooperation of the people. The reason civilian support efforts are so important in the 2nd Operational Command area during peacetime is to secure the support of the residents in times of emergency. When natural disasters occur, the military takes the lead in recovery efforts for the same reason.

There were many underprivileged children at the orphanage waiting for a warm helping hand. Helping local orphanages through soldiers' campaigns to support neighbors in need was undoubtedly a top priority. Soldiers with the ability to provide academic guidance were selected to teach the underprivileged children, and surplus materials were gathered to repair the orphanage facilities. At times, due to soldiers being away on leave or overnight stays, there was a surplus of rice. Sending the remaining rice to the orphanage was a great help in supplementing the nutrition of the growing children.

With children from an orphanage

The official residence of the 2nd Operational Command, built among Himalayan cedar trees, resembled a villa. Waking up in the morning to the beautiful sound of birdsong, the refreshing air added to the sense of vitality. Next to the residence was a church. As soon as I woke up, I would take my Bible and head out for early morning prayer, brushing past the dew-covered grass, feeling completely invigorated. After the prayer, I would jog along the wooded trail of the golf course inside the base to build up my physical strength. A refreshing shower after sweating rejuvenated me completely, and I would begin the workday with doubled efficiency.

Because of the children's education, I was living alone in Daegu, separated from my family. On weekends or holidays, my family would come down from Seoul. The times when they visited were the happiest and most joyful. Although the special nature of military life had made us a separated family, I came to realize that being with my family also improved my work performance. Frequent relocations as a soldier made it difficult to provide a stable education for my children, but they grew up to be upright on their own, for which I, as a parent, could not be more grateful.

My family at Halla Mountain
(from left: the author, Cha Soo-jin, Kim Kyeong-ah, Cha Jeong-seok)

Cha Soo-jin, who is growing up at her maternal grandparents' house, often felt like someone else's daughter because we couldn't meet frequently. To give her the affection I couldn't usually provide, we would go on family trips during my leave. We traveled to Jeju Island for the first time since our honeymoon. Jeju Island had a military resort, so we were able to travel at a relatively low cost. Although my wife, who wasn't in the best health, struggled during the climb up Halla Mountain, it became a hiking trip we would remember for a long time.

Engaging in leisure activities such as tennis, horseback riding, and skiing with my family was also a source of happiness. I wasn't good at these sports from the start, but I learned them as hobbies, step by step, together with my family. It was during this time that Cha Soo-jin and Cha Jeong-seok developed a love for skiing. The children, who, like me, didn't have much natural talent for sports, progressed to an expert level.

3. My Connection with the 37th Division

December 29, 1991!

With my promotion to major general, I was appointed as the commander of the 37th Division. It is said that the position of division commander is the "flower" of the military. This is because it guarantees the conditions to directly oversee the combat forces and freely command the unit. As the strongest unit capable of integrated arms operations, and the best combat force where one can work closely with the soldiers, it is a position that everyone wants to experience at least once.

The 37th Division is located in Jeungpyeong, Chungcheongbuk-do, and holds the crucial mission of guarding the Baekdu Mountain Range, including the Jukryung, Ihwaryung, and Chupungryung Pass. The previous division commander was

General Park Soon-chan (the 21st Class of KMA). It was a great honor for me to take over the elite division that General Park had meticulously built.

Many alumni from the Korea Military Academy and high school attended the division commander's inauguration ceremony. Relatives and family members from Daegu also attended. I was grateful for the friends, relatives, and colleagues who came from far away to congratulate me. The inauguration took place with many distinguished guests, including the 9th Corps Commander, the Governor of Chungcheongbuk-do, local officials, and commanders from neighboring units, as I took office as the 25th Commander of the 37th Division.

Inauguration ceremony of the 37th Division Commander

After the inauguration ceremony, a reception followed. In foreign countries, such events are usually focused on the incoming commander, but in the Korean military, both the departing and incoming commanders are given attention. To ensure no one feels left out, both the person leaving and the one arriving are bid farewell and welcomed together.

Reception after the inauguration ceremony
(From right to left my wife, the author)

My father-in-law and mother-in-law at the inauguration ceremony.

The 37th Infantry Division holds a special connection for me, as my father-in-law, General Kim Seon-gyu, served as its 10th division commander. While serving as the 37th Division commander, I worked hard to develop the division into one of the best. General Kim Seon-gyu attended my inauguration ceremony and, as he reminisced about the past, he was filled with emotion.

The local residents recognized my father-in-law, General Kim Seon-gyu, who had been a former division commander, and were very pleased to see him. General Kim, who was especially compassionate, had a deep affection for the residents of Chungcheongbuk-do. Having two generations of our family serve as division commanders in the beautiful region of Chungcheong-do, known for its scenic landscapes and historical charm, felt as if we had a deep connection to this land from a past life. Though time had passed, the people's warmth and the charm of this land in the heart of Chungcheong remained unchanged. The division had a large pond, and it was a touching sight to see my father-in-law and mother-in-law sitting on the pavilion by the pond or on the grass of the commander's yard, reminiscing about the past. My wife, Kim Kyeong-ah, who had grown up in the division's commander's residence, was happier than anyone else when I was appointed the 37th Division Commander. Returning to that house, that building, and that yard filled her with overwhelming emotions.

I first emphasized unit cohesion upon assuming command of the division. To control the widely scattered units across the vast operational area, it was necessary to instill a sense of attachment to the division in every soldier. To unify the division, I created a division anthem that embodied the spirit of the unit. I wrote the lyrics and gave them to the division's bandmaster with an order to compose the music. Major Jeong Jin-seop, the bandmaster, consulted with experts and set my lyrics to music, creating the *Chungyongga* (song of loyalty and valor).

Chungyongga (Division Anthem)

Young souls of loyalty and valor
stationed in the Baekdu Mountains
The shield of a nation, firmly united like steel
Who could ever stand against them
Incarnations of the immortal phoenix
Their name will forever live on
The warriors of the Chungyong Division.

An unyielding belief that burns like a torch
An invincible spirit, honed
Sharpened through training
Who could dare cross the line

My homeland, my land

Their name will forever live on

The warriors of the Chungyong Division.

Receiving a situation report
(Front row, from left: Deputy Division Commander Yeo Gil-do, the author)

Upon assuming command of the division, I found that the staff officers and senior commanders were all excellent. Since the division was close to the capital region, there were three Deputy Division Commanders: Colonel Yeo Gil-do (the 21st Class of KMA), Colonel Choi Hak, and Colonel Lee Tae-hee. Colonel Yeo Gil-do was a kind senior who had taught and mentored me during my time as a cadet. Along with the regimental commanders, including Colonel Kim Hyun-seok (who later became the head of Korea Military Academy), they all worked hard to develop the division under the leadership of the division commander. The division commander did not lead from his office but instead spent most of his time in the field, visiting subordinate units to provide guidance. He practiced the principle of 5% planning and 95% supervision through his actions.

During the operation guidance for subordinate units.

The division commander was provided with two helicopters for command. Since the operational area was vast, it was not possible to travel everywhere by vehicle. The commander used the helicopter to visit subordinate units and provide operational guidance. The division commander personally conducted morale training for the soldiers, as strengthening mental fortitude is a crucial factor in winning battles. At the battalion-level tactical training grounds, the division commander directly checked to ensure that the training was practical and realistic. A soldier must always be prepared with the mindset that war could break out at any moment. The core of combat readiness begins with training that mirrors real combat situations.

On July 8, 1994, North Korean leader Kim Il-sung passed away from a heart attack. An order to strengthen combat readiness was issued across the entire military. Since North Korea had been under a long-standing, one-man dictatorship, the sudden death of its leader raised concerns about what might happen next. The division maintained full combat readiness and prepared for any potential real-world situation.

Whenever the division commander visited the training ground, the subordinate commanders would prepare chairs and tables, carefully considering what kind of food the commander liked and what type of tea he preferred. If it became known that the division commander liked oxtail soup, oxtail soup would be prepared everywhere he went. Similarly, if he drank ginseng tea due to a cold, every unit would have ginseng tea ready for him.

It took considerable time to eliminate this practice. In the field, I strictly prohibited the preparation of chairs and tables.

I instructed the soldiers to report while sitting on the ground, as they were. In cases where it was absolutely necessary, a field chair might be provided, but they were thoroughly trained to report to the division commander under conditions similar to those in a wartime situation. Meals were taken in the field with the soldiers' rations, and I made sure that no special food for the division commander was prepared in a separate dining facility. In a wartime scenario, when would there be time to prepare meals or tea? If possible, I made sure that only interchangeable combat rations were prepared.

The Korean military has a weakness in that officers do not experience enlisted military service before commissioning. In contrast, the North Korean military selects officers from among the enlisted soldiers, which means that all officers are well-acquainted with the world of enlisted personnel. However, in the Korean military, officers commissioned from KMA, ROTC, and the 3rd Military Academy do not have experience in enlisted military service, which leads to a lack of understanding of the enlisted soldiers' world.

In order to experience enlisted military service firsthand, I lived with the enlisted soldiers at the most remote post, called the Jukryeong post. At first, the officers were uncomfortable with this arrangement. The enlisted soldiers also found it difficult to have the division commander spend time in their barracks. However, as time went by, a sense of camaraderie began to develop between the division commander and the enlisted soldiers.

Sharing the experiences of enlisted military service

The division commander spent 2 nights and 3 days at each of the Jukryeong, Iwharyeong, and Chupungryeong posts, living alongside the enlisted soldiers. The Baekdu Mountain Range had been a strategic area on the Korean Peninsula even before the Korean War due to the threat of enemy infiltration. The division's top priority was to strengthen the defense of this region. All support was focused on these posts. Sharing meals with the soldiers in the same way became second nature. I would stand in line at the mess hall and receive food like the soldiers. Sleeping and bathing together were no longer awkward. With all decision-making delegated to the Deputy Division Commander, the division commander was able to fully experience enlisted military service without any interruptions from the staff. While the military principle is that officers and soldiers should be distinct, it was believed that spending a period of time living alongside the soldiers as part of experiencing enlisted military service was also necessary.

I am watching the raising of the Outstanding Unit Flag.

Competition was encouraged between units to maximize combat effectiveness and achieve perfect unit management.

Outstanding units in combat performance and accident-free units were selected and given awards and encouragement. When units are made to compete, they will strive harder than any other group. Every six months, the best units in each category were selected, and their flags were raised high in front of the division headquarters for everyone to see. Since the military is a group that thrives on honor, each unit eagerly hoped to see its flag displayed at the division headquarters for the honor of their unit.

Whenever the flag of their own unit was raised at the division headquarters, the soldiers of that unit would look at it with pride and satisfaction every time they visited the division. The model of raising the flag of the outstanding unit through competition was one of the effective methods for enhancing the combat power of the units.

On January 7, 1993, at 01:13 AM, a large fire broke out in a commercial building in downtown Cheongju. The Uam Shopping Center in Sangdang-gu, Cheongju, collapsed, resulting in the deaths of 28 residents and injuries to 48 others. Additionally, 74 shops, including grocery stores and clothing stores, located on the basement and first floors, were completely destroyed. The collapse of the apartments on the second to fourth floors left 59 households completely devastated, and more than 350 people became displaced.1

Woken up in the middle of the night, the division commander received a report from the situation officer and immediately put on combat attire, rushing to the scene. Realizing the severity of the situation, the division deployed all available personnel and equipment to the scene. The military possesses quick responsiveness. Thanks to this quick response in the initial operation, the division's equipment and personnel arrived at the scene faster than the fire trucks.

I am inspecting the recovery site of the Uam Shopping Center with Deputy Division Commander Colonel Choi Hak.

---

1   The Chosun Ilbo, January 8, 1993

Protecting the lives and property of the people is the fundamental duty of the military. Just as military operations in war are crucial to defeating the enemy, it is only natural for the military to be deployed in disaster recovery operations. The division, which achieved success in the swift initial response, appointed Deputy Division Commander Colonel Choi Hak as the on-site commander for ongoing recovery efforts and received great praise from the public.

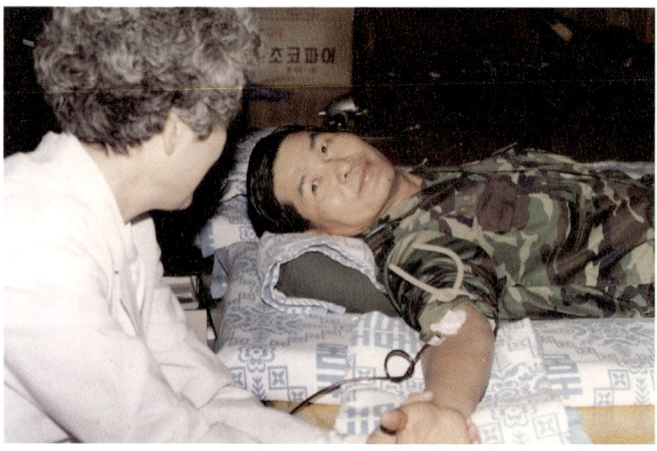

Donating blood

As many casualties occurred, there was a shortage of blood. Patients waiting for transfusions lined up at hospitals, but the limited blood supply was insufficient to meet the demand. The division commander took the lead and donated blood. Having donated blood more than twice a year as usual, I called the head of the Cheongju Red Cross to the unit to organize a blood donation drive. With the division commander taking the lead, all personnel in the division followed suit and joined in.

The shortage of blood was completely resolved by the young blood of the soldiers of the 37th Division. Praise and encouragement for the division's efficient and dedicated Cheongju market recovery efforts poured in from local media, as well as from national news outlets. A military that stands with the people can also win against the enemy. Especially since support activities for local residents can directly influence combat effectiveness in times of emergency, these activities become a key factor in enhancing military combat power.

Our division soldiers took the lead in environmental protection efforts within our operational area. In the land of scenic landscapes, trash and waste left behind by tourists had polluted various spots. The contamination was even more severe at famous tourist destinations such as the Namhan River, Huayang Valley, Chungju Lake, and Daecheong Lake. Not only was the drinking water for the citizens of Seoul, Cheongju, and Daejeon being polluted, but the Baekdu Mountain Range was also turning into a dumping ground for garbage.

During the environmental protection movement around the Namhan River

The division commander took the initiative in the trash collection efforts and instructed all subordinate units to also take the lead in environmental protection. Utilizing available personnel and equipment, they thoroughly cleaned up even the debris deeply buried in the rivers and lakes. Soldiers, once discharged, become citizens of the nation. The environmental protection movement they participated in during their active duty can lead to a change in habits, such as refraining from littering and protecting nature after their service. The military's environmental protection efforts can serve as an effective form of public education, shaping future citizens.

Non-commissioned officers are the backbone of the military.

They play a key role as a bridge between officers and enlisted soldiers, making them a vital military component. However, the use and attention given to non-commissioned officers have generally been insufficient. There was a tendency to think of non-commissioned officers as an ineffective and unmotivated group.

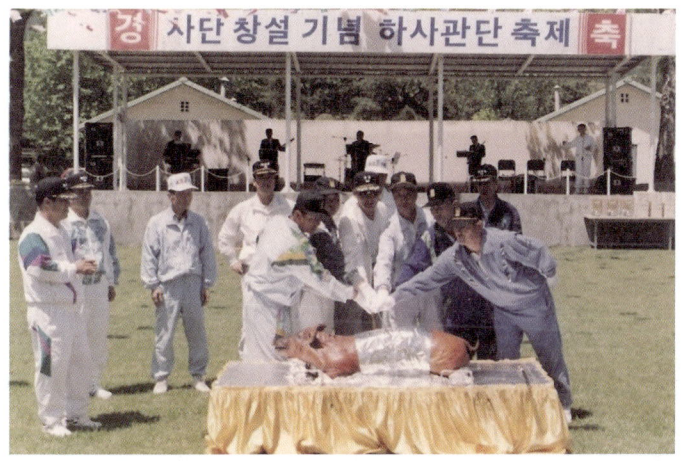

Cutting the barbecue at the non-commissioned officers' festival

In order to break these misconceptions, I actively utilized non-commissioned officers. I assigned tasks that matched their abilities, granting them the corresponding authority and responsibility. I created an atmosphere where enlisted soldiers trusted and followed their non-commissioned officers. On all formal occasions, I placed the division sergeant major on the same level as the division commander. While officers serve for a limited period before leaving the unit, non-commissioned officers stay with the same unit for a long time, becoming the true owners and driving forces of the unit. I organized non-commissioned officers' festivals, such as on the division's anniversary, to boost their morale and motivation.

Having a conversation with Unbo Kim Ki-chang, a renowned artist

Visiting a nursing home in the operational area

Within the division's operational area was the villa of the world-renowned painter, Kim Ki-chang, known as Unbo. The portrait of King Sejong, which appears on the 10,000-won bill, was also painted by Kim Ki-chang in his studio at the villa. I had the opportunity to visit him in his later years, engaging in conversations that allowed me to learn about both his artwork and the person behind Unbo. As the division commander, I was able to offer him some comfort in his old age.

I frequently visited nursing homes and orphanages. I reached out to elderly grandparents with no one to rely on and orphaned children, offering them comfort and support. There were many such unfortunate facilities within the operational area. Being close to the capital region and surrounded by the beautiful, fresh air and clean water of the scenic landscapes, it was an area with many nursing homes and orphanages.

My mother, who had been at my eldest brother's house in Daegu, came to the division commander's residence. To show filial piety, which had been difficult to do for a long time, a grand celebration for the elderly in the area was held with my mother. Since it was the first time a division commander personally hosted a feast for the elderly, the local residents were very pleased. It became clear that gaining the trust and confidence of the people was one of the ways to enhance combat readiness.

The Flower Village, located within the division area, was a great place for both volunteer activities by our division soldiers and as a mental training ground. Flower Village is a paradise for the underprivileged, established by Father Oh Woong-jin on November 15, 1976, after he was moved by the good deeds of an elderly beggar named Choi Gwi-dong. This place, where people abandoned by society gather, accommodates individuals ranging from infants to 100-year-old grandmothers. Visiting this place gives a sense that one's perspective on life changes.

Flower Village

I went to meet Father Oh Woong-jin at Flower Village and saw a person without arms or legs, with a bright face, organizing my shoes at the entrance. This person said that organizing the shoes of visitors at the entrance was his duty. When I heard his story, he told me that he had gone to the Middle East for work, but his wife had taken all the money he had sent and run away with another man. In his anger, he made a homemade grenade and threw it at the couple who had fled, but it accidentally went off and blew off his arms and legs. For a while, he wanted to die, but after turning to religion, he let go of all his resentment and now lives with gratitude for everything. He said he was thankful just to be alive and was living a happy life with a bright face. I was deeply moved by seeing the people living in Flower Village, who, despite their misfortune, always lived with gratitude and joy, smiling.

Soldiers in our division were required to volunteer at Flower Village as soon as they enlisted. As a result, the unit became an accident-free division and was recognized as the best combat unit, even receiving the Presidential Citation. During my tenure as division commander, the 37th Division was the only one to receive the Presidential Citation twice.

4. Defense Secretary to the Blue House

On October 18, 1994, General Kim Dong-jin, the Army Chief of Staff, called me up to come to his office at Army Headquarters. It was rare for the Army Chief of Staff to summon a division commander. While conducting field training, I couldn't even change my clothes and went straight to the Army

Chief of Staff's office.

"General Cha ! Would you like to work as Defense Secretary at the Blue House?"

"Yes! I will do my best."

It was near the end of my two-year term as division commander, so I was curious about my next assignment. Since I had only worked in the field until then, serving in a policy department was a desirable opportunity.

When the rumor spread that I would be going to serve as Defense Secretary to the Blue House, congratulatory calls came from all directions. After serving as a division commander, the Blue House was a place everyone wanted to work at least once. Leaving behind the deep affection built up over two years in the division, I headed to the Blue House.

Upon entering the unfamiliar doors of the Blue House, Jeong Jong-wook, the Senior Secretary for Foreign Affairs and Security, warmly welcomed me. Jeong Jong-wook, born in 1940, had earned a Ph.D. in political science and diplomacy from Yale University and was a professor at Seoul National University before serving as Senior Secretary for Foreign Affairs and Security under the Kim Young-sam administration.

Meeting President Kim Young-sam after being appointed as the Defense Secretary to the Blue House

Under the Senior Secretary for Foreign Affairs and Security were the Secretaries for Foreign Affairs, Defense, and Unification. At that time, the Foreign Affairs Secretary was Yu Myung-hwan (later Minister of Foreign Affairs), the Unification Secretary was Chung Sae-hyun (later Minister of Unification), and I was appointed as the Defense Secretary. The three of us were called the troika for Korea's diplomacy, security, and unification. Since there was no National Security Office head system at the time, all security affairs were handled by the Defense Secretary.

The Defense Secretary was the highest position for an active-duty officer, responsible for drafting major defense policies and assisting the president while maintaining organic communication and control with the Ministry of National Defense and the headquarters of each military branch. The staff at the Defense Secretary's office were also selected from the top elite officers of the Army, Navy, Air Force, and Marine Corps. For the Army, Colonel Kim Kwan-jin (later Minister of National Defense) and Colonel Kim Tae-young (later Minister of National Defense) were assigned; for the Navy, Colonel Choi Yoon-hee (later Chairman of the Joint Chiefs of Staff); and for the Air Force, Colonel Kim Hyung-chul, among others. These officers were recognized as outstanding in both ability and character within their branches and were guaranteed promotion in the future.

Staff of the Blue House Defense Secretary's Office
(I am standing fourth from the left)

At that time, a policy was established to recruit female cadets to the military academy. Until then, the military academy was considered a forbidden place for women, and they were not allowed to enter. However, since the role of women in the military was increasing in modern warfare, the policy was formulated to recruit female cadets.

It took time to persuade the Army. They said the frontline field areas were not ready to accommodate female soldiers. It was difficult because separate facilities such as dormitories and restrooms for women had not been prepared. However, after continuously persuading the military academy principal, female cadets were eventually recruited in intervals of one year each, starting with the Air Force, then the Army, and finally the Navy.

As a result of implementing the female cadet system through these difficult processes, the role of women in the military greatly improved. Outstanding resources were commissioned as female officers, to the extent that top graduates of the military academy and excellent graduates of various military training courses were all women. They have made significant contributions to enhancing our military's combat power.

The Blue House has a Yeonmugwan (training hall). Although it is a facility for security staff, all Blue House personnel could use it. The secretaries formed a Keomdo club and practiced Keomdo every dawn.

First dan in keomdo (I am standing second from the left.)

Traffic congestion in Seoul was severe during rush hours. I left home early in the morning when the roads were relatively clear and practiced Keomdo at Yeonmugwan to avoid the crowded times. After exercising, I showered and had a simple breakfast at the cafeteria before going to the office. As a result of exercising every day without fail, by the time I completed my two-year term as Defense Secretary, I was able to earn a first dan in Keomdo. With a second dan in Judo, a fifth dan in Hapkido, and a first dan in Keomdo, I completed the martial arts required of a warrior.

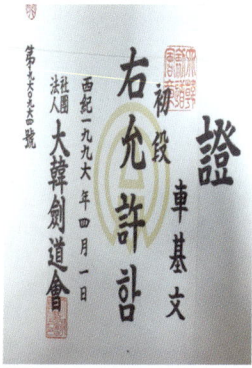 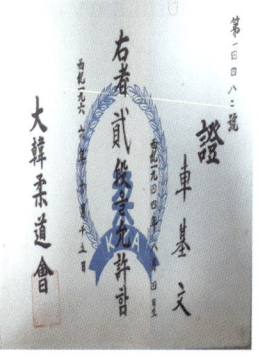 

First dan in keomdo   Second dan in judo   Fifth dan in hapkido

Secretaries organized the Cheongsanhoe (Blue House Hiking Club) every week, led by Chief Secretary Han Seung-soo (later Prime Minister). Han Seung-soo loved the mountains so much that it was said he could fly around when hiking. On overseas trips, he was known for strengthening his stamina by climbing up and down the stairs of 100-story buildings.

He possessed both virtue and intelligence, earning the full respect and trust of all of us secretaries. Although most hikes were focused on Bukhansan Mountain, sometimes we undertook long-distance hikes, strengthening our physical fitness and camaraderie with the Chief Secretary. As a result of Keomdo training and Hiking, not only was a healthy physical condition maintained, but work efficiency also improved within the united atmosphere. Serving at the Blue House was a rewarding time that combined both civil and military duties.

Cheongsanhoe (the author and Chief Secretary Han Seung-soo in the front row)

Horseback riding

I rode horses. A riding stable near the Korea Military Academy owned 30 horses. When first starting horseback riding, the groin area was bruised dark blue. Even riding for just one hour would soak the entire body in sweat. Riding skills were learned in the order of walk, trot, and canter, and daily interest in horseback riding grew.

The time as Defense Secretary at the Blue House was meaningful not only because of the rewarding work but also because it allowed for various hobbies.

5. DCS of the ROK/US Combined Forces Command & Senior Member of the Military Armistice Commission

On July 30, 1996, after completing the President Defense Secretary role at the Blue House, I was assigned as the Deputy Chief of Staff of the ROK/US Combined Forces Command and concurrently as the senior member to the Military Armistice Commission. I was the right candidate because I could communicate in English with U.S. forces and had extensive experience in ROK/US combined operations. The Deputy

Chief of Staff of the ROK/US Combined Forces Command also served as the senior representative to the Military Armistice Commission. The Military Armistice Commission belongs to the United Nations Command to maintain and manage the armistice agreement. The United Nations Command has been managed by the United States since July 7, 1950, based on United Nations Security Council Resolution 84. It organizes multinational forces to respond to threats in case of Korean Peninsula.

For this purpose, there are seven United Nations Command rear bases in Japan (Yokota, Zama, Yokosuka, Sasebo, Kadena, Futenma, and White). These bases are prepared for the return of U.S. forces and third-country troops in case of war on the Korean Peninsula. They are fully equipped with the necessary capabilities and facilities to serve as storage sites for United Nations Command military supplies and as intermediate bases.

In modern warfare, the role of multinational forces is extremely important. If North Korea were to start a war again, a multinational force could be formed immediately centered on the 16 UN participating countries according to the Washington Declaration of July 27, 1953. However, there are some negative views about the United Nations Command within Korean society. If the United Nations Command were to be disbanded, it would be impossible to recreate it and form a multinational force again, because China and Russia are likely to oppose the reestablishment of the United Nations Command.

The Military Armistice Commission was composed of forces from South and North Korea, the United Nations Command, and China. The senior representative of the communist forces was Lieutenant General Lee Chan-bok of the North Korean army, while I served as the senior representative for the United Nations Command. The Chief of Staff of the ROK/US Combined Forces Command was a U.S. Army lieutenant general, whereas the corresponding Korean chief of staff, that is, the Deputy Chief of Staff of the ROK/US Combined Forces Command, held the rank of major general. Having me as the Deputy Chief of Staff of the ROK/US Combined Forces Command and Senior Representative of the Military Armistice Commission at the rank of major general was unbalanced in terms of parity with the U.S. forces and the communist side.

To resolve this imbalance, the Blue House and the Ministry of National Defense decided to promote me to lieutenant general. I was promoted to lieutenant general 29 years after graduating from the military academy. In the military, promotion step by step is crucial for one's career because failure to be promoted means having to retire.

The President and the Minister of National Defense are pinning the lieutenant general rank insignia on me.

Not everyone who graduates from the Korea Military Academy becomes a general. Promotion requires ability as well as some degree of luck. Among the 23rd class of the Korea Military Academy, only 28% of the total graduates became generals. Among them, there were only eight lieutenant generals. Among those eight lieutenant generals, Lee Nam-shin and Kim Seok-jae were promoted to general. General Lee Nam-shin was recognized for his outstanding ability from his cadet days, having received the United Nations Commander's Award upon graduation from the academy. General Kim Seok-jae was also a competent general, possessing both wisdom and virtue, and was highly respected by his classmates.

Upon promotion to lieutenant general, President Kim Young-sam personally pinned the rank insignia on me and presented a samjeongdo with the presidential emblem attached. When becoming a general, the Samjeongdo is awarded by the president, and with each subsequent promotion, a ribbon is added to the Samjeongdo. My promotion to lieutenant general was not only due to good fortune but also thanks to the dedicated sacrifices of my classmates and God's blessing.

With my promotion to lieutenant general, having led the ROK/US combined operations, I established operational plan 5027, reflecting the will and objectives of the Korean military. The ROK/US Combined Forces Command was staffed equally by Korean and U.S. forces, each holding 50% of the positions. All planning and unit operations were decided jointly. The increased voice of the Korean military and the active reflection of our will in the operational plan were due to the growth of our national power.

In the early days, when Korea's national power was greatly lacking, there was complete reliance on the U.S. military, but as

Korea's national power grew, the status of the Korean military rose proportionally. Initially, training costs, food expenses, and administrative supplies depended on U.S. military support. At that time, the Korean forces were often looked down upon by the U.S. military, which hurt their pride. There were many occasions when Korean opinions were not reflected in operational plan drafting, leading to frequent conflicts with the U.S. forces.

However, as our national power grew, the Korean military was able to take a leading role in all aspects. The U.S. forces did not know the terrain, weather and unit structure in Korea better than the Korean military. The military education and English skills of Korean officers also improved. Work could be carried out not just on an equal footing but proactively.

In particular, Randy House, the U.S. Eighth Army commander and my American counterpart, was a close friend I had known since we were junior officers as classmates at the U.S. Army Command and General Staff College. We were the same age and held the same rank of lieutenant general, so cooperation and collaboration went very smoothly in every aspect.

In order to ensure smooth official business between the ROK and the U.S., informal personal relationships were also one of the very important factors. General Randy House, the U.S.

Eighth Army commander and the deputy chief of staff of the ROK/US Combined Forces Command, was from Texas and liked horseback riding. He owned 150 horses on his ranch back home. Having ridden horses since childhood, he walked with a bowlegged gait. Since I also had a hobby of horseback riding at the Korea Military Academy riding grounds in Taereung, we further strengthened our friendship by riding together during our leisure time.

Leading combined operations with U.S. generals

Present the command baton to Randy House, U.S. Eighth Army commander

My wife taught General Randy House's wife, Jeany, about Korean culture, traditions, and customs. She taught pottery at the Yeoju ceramics factory and introduced Korean mask dances and traditional games at the folk village. For the Lunar New Year holiday, she had a hanbok tailored for the House couple, and whenever there was an event, they appeared dressed in a hanbok to show their gratitude to us.

From the left: the author, Kim Kyeong-ah, Jeany, General Randy House, U.S. Eighth Army commander

As informal exchanges increased and the friendship deepened, trust between the Korea and the U.S. grew even stronger. When conducting combined ROK/US operations, we went out to the field together to provide guidance. General Randy House was in charge of U.S. tactics, while I instructed the U.S. forces on Korean tactics. Since the training was preparation for war in Korea, the Korean aspects were more prominent. Although the

U.S. forces had extensive combat experience in Europe and the Middle East, they were unfamiliar with the mountainous terrain of Korea. In Korea's terrain, which required infantry-focused operations rather than tank warfare, my advice and guidance were especially necessary. The close personal relationship with my partner, General Randy House, made the combined ROK/US operations more efficient.

FOAL EAGLE DRILL—Lt. Gen. Cha Ki-moon, deputy chief of staff at the ROK-U.S. Combined Forces Command, and U.S. officers inspect a training site near Tongduchon, north of Seoul, where Foal Eagle '98 field training exercise was underway yesterday.
Yonhap

Newspaper coverage showing the author (center) instructing U.S. forces during training

The Military Armistice Commission consisted of five representatives each from the UN forces and the Communist forces. On the UN side, I served as the senior representative, with representatives from the United States, the United Kingdom, and other participating countries attending. On the Communist side, the senior representative was from the North Korean army, with the commission composed of both Chinese and North Korean forces.

Under me, serving as the senior representative of the United Nations Command, were U.S. Major General Michael V. Hayden, British Brigadier General Colin Parr, and colonels representing the 16 UN member states that had participated in the Korean War. General Hayden later returned to the United States and served as Director of the CIA under President Bush. I was able to maintain a long-standing friendship with him, and among all, General Hayden and his wife were especially warm and personable.

With MG Michael V. Hayden, who was nominated as Director of the CIA, and his wife

As the senior representative of the Military Armistice Commission, I was primarily responsible for the affairs of the United Nations Command. General John Tilleli, the commander of U.S. Forces Korea who concurrently served as the commander of the United Nations Command, was holding as many as seven different posts, so he had no time to be involved in the operations of the United Nations Command. All subordinate units of the United Nations Command, except for U.S. forces, had already withdrawn. Even among U.S. forces, only a small number of personnel remained, such as the security guards and honor guard stationed at Panmunjom.

With the establishment of the ROK/US Combined Forces Command, the core missions of the United Nations Command were to maintain and manage the armistice agreement and to receive third-country troops in case of emergency. Under my supervision, the U.S. and U.K. representatives to the Military Armistice Commission, who were assigned as generals, along with representatives from other participating nations, held weekly meetings to discuss matters related to the United Nations Command. The United Nations Command needed to be properly managed in peacetime in order to be prepared to receive third-country troops in the event of an emergency.

The Neutral Nations Supervisory Commission (NNSC), which monitored violations of the Armistice Agreement, was also under my jurisdiction. On the United Nations side, Switzerland and Sweden participated, while Poland and Czechoslovakia represented the communist side. However, starting in April 1993, North Korea forcibly expelled the representatives from Poland and Czechoslovakia. Their intention was to neutralize the Armistice Agreement and engage in direct talks with the United States.

Presiding over the UNC meeting | I am the white dress uniform in the center.

As a result, the NNSC, which had set up a camp in Panmunjom to monitor violations of the Armistice Agreement, was effectively paralyzed. The NNSC personnel from the communist side had no choice but to come to Seoul and carry out duties related to the Armistice Agreement together with the UN NNSC personnel. The Polish and Czechoslovakian representatives, who had been expelled from North Korea, continued to fulfill their essential responsibilities from Seoul. North Korea, by disregarding the Armistice Agreement along with all other international treaties, brought diplomatic isolation upon itself. In contrast, South Korea made every effort to uphold the existing Armistice Agreement until a new one could be established, striving for stability and peace on the Korean Peninsula.

Visiting the U.S. 7th Fleet my wife, Kim Kyeong-ah in Yokosuka, Japan

I made regular visits to the United Nations Command rear headquarters in Japan, accompanied by United Nations

Command officers. I visited the U.S. Fifth Air Force Headquarters in Yokota, the U.S. Seventh Fleet Headquarters in Yokosuka, and the U.S. Marine Corps Headquarters in Okinawa to routinely check the operational readiness of the U.S. Forces in Japan.

As the U.S.-Japan alliance was strengthened under the new U.S.-Japan Security Treaty, the relationship between the United Nations Command and Japan also became closer. Whenever I visited the United Nations Command rear headquarters, I received briefings on the current status of the Japan Self-Defense Forces and the Defense Agency. It provided an opportunity to study what role Japan would play in the event of a war on the Korean Peninsula.

Yutnori with United Nations Command personnel
(I am wearing a hanbok in the center)

To carry out the United Nations Command's duties efficiently and effectively, friendly relations with representatives of the participating countries were important. Introducing and familiarizing foreigners with Korea's culture, customs, history, and traditions was also part of preparing for combat readiness in the war.

During holidays, I taught them Korea's unique customs by playing yutnori, jegichagi, and kite flying. Just like the proverb, "When in Rome, do as the Romans do," I emphasized that foreigners visiting Korea should follow Korean culture and customs, making efforts to help them understand Korea. They greatly liked Korea's fine traditions. Even with yutnori alone, creating various rules made it more interesting than any other game.

Unlike Koreans, foreigners were not good at singing. To help them adapt to our customs, they were often taken to karaoke rooms. At first, they were reluctant, saying they couldn't sing. However, by steadily teaching them songs and dances, they gradually adapted to our culture and later became even more enthusiastic. They repeatedly urged me to go to karaoke despite my busy schedule. Through this informal exchange, camaraderie within the United Nations Command was strengthened, and trust was built. Through trust and faith, the combat readiness for war was also fully prepared.

Kim Joo-hyeuk

Cha Soo-jin

On January 9, 1999, Cha Soo-jin got married. Cha Soo-jin, who had said she would not marry even if set up by a matchmaker, one day came with her boyfriend and declared she would get married.

The young man was Kim Joo-hyeuk, who graduated from the Department of Mechanical Engineering at Seoul National University College of Engineering. He made a good first impression and seemed to be a capable young man with a promising future. He was kind-hearted and an elite raised in a prestigious family with proper upbringing. Above all, it was important that the two parties liked each other. My wife and I believed that no matter how well parents introduced someone, if the individuals themselves did not want it, it would not work.

Kim Joo-hyeuk and
Cha Soo-jin's wedding

Parents of both families at wedding

At Hartel House, the generals' dining hall of the ROK/US Combined Forces Command, both families met for a formal introduction, and the in-laws were also excellent people with modern mindsets. The woman who was to become Cha Soo-jin's sister-in-law graduated from Ewha Womans University Medical College and was a distinguished doctor combining both refinement and integrity. Her husband, Cha Soo-jin's brother-in-law, worked as a lawyer at a well-known law firm and was a competent legal professional recognized for his trustworthiness and ability.

The son-in-law, Kim Joo-hyeuk, was working at the head office of Korea's top automobile company. Coincidentally, General Min Seong-gi, a classmate of my Korea Military Academy, was his superior there. When I asked General Min to check on Kim Joo-hyeuk, his evaluation was even more favorable than I had thought.

After all preparations were complete, the wedding ceremony was held at the Army Officers' Club in Yongsan. General Min Seong-gi officiated the ceremony. There were many guests since both families were having their first child marriage. Seeing the harmonious couple brought me a renewed sense of what happiness truly is.

6. Departing from Active Duty

September 29, 2000!

After 37 years of wearing a uniform, including time at the military academy, retirement was official. The retirement ceremony was held at the parade ground of the 37th Division, a unit I had the deepest attachment to, surrounded by seniors, juniors, colleagues, relatives, and family. The following passage, sent by my friend Kim Ki-bong who attended the ceremony, describes the scene at that time.

On the day General Cha Kimoon retired,

On the afternoon of Friday, September 29, 2000, it seemed the weather forecast predicting rain in the central region had been mistaken. Under the clear, high autumn sky, with cotton-ball clouds scattered across, the still-warm sunlight adorned the noses of the soldiers standing on the parade ground with tiny jade-like beads.

The parade ground of the 37th Infantry Division, nestled on the low slopes near Jeungpyeong Field close to Cheongju in Chungcheong Province, featured soldiers fully equipped in combat gear standing in formation on the fine grass that resembled a golf course fairway. They stood at attention, motionless, watching the red three-star Army flag and numerous general officers' flags fluttering at both ends of the reviewing stand.

With the fanfare of the military band breaking the silence, the black car adorned with a red three-star insignia arrived at the reviewing stand, and the three-star general and his spouse stepped out! The stars on the general's shoulders dazzled in the early autumn sunlight, the numerous medals on his chest looked as abundant as the late autumn harvest, and the general's eyes reflected tender memories like images shimmering on a calm lake.

> Personnel Order No. 127
>
> Lieutenant General Cha Kimoon of the Army, having served the nation and people with a noble spirit of patriotism and loyalty for 37 years, is honorably discharged and transferred to the Republic of Korea Army Reserve.
>
> September 29, 2000
>
> President Kim Dae-jung

Though it was hard to believe that the long journey of 37 years, full of glory, honor, and anguish, was ending with a single personnel order, perhaps it was the sense of duty to return the single personnel order received at Hwarangdae 37 years ago back to the nation. As the general and his wife rode up to the review stand and received salutes from the soldiers, the autumn breeze gently brushed over their calm expressions.

The general reflected, "From being born as the son of an ordinary farmer to today, when I conclude my military service… just the honor of being promoted to army lieutenant general, a rank not given to just anyone, made my life truly happy and fulfilling." As he recalled precious memories such as his cadet days when he willingly chose the difficult path of justice over the easy path of injustice, his time as a platoon leader executing counter guerrilla operations across the Taebaek mountain range, and his days as a young officer navigating life-and-death moments in the jungles of Vietnam war, his expression, as if engraving these memories in his heart, seemed to tremble.

The general, satisfied, said, "The military life I chose for myself was a proud and regret-free time during which I strived and endured to fulfill my duties and responsibilities as a true and honorable soldier." All the guests and soldiers present gave him endless looks of admiration and respect for a successful life.

Recalling the warnings of the world's great scholars—"Be cautious of danger when the ice thaws, and if you desire peace, prepare for war"—the general did not forget to express his hopes and admonitions regarding the current national situation, which is captivated by illusions of unification. He said, "For our nation to be freed from the fear of war and for peaceful reunification of the North and South to be achieved, a strong and robust national security must be firmly supported." Then, removing the blue uniform that symbolized 37 years of honor and glory, he said, "I take off the uniform I have worn for 37 years and, as an ordinary citizen, I depart as a veteran, cherishing precious memories."

At the command of "Attention, salute to Lieutenant General Cha Kimoon!" from the commanding officers and unit leaders, the resounding "Loyalty" rang out, accompanied by the military band's lively melody honoring the three-star general. This final salute echoed into the blue sky like a fading reverberation.

The current division commander, proposing a toast with the guests gathered in the reception hall, introduced as follows: "General Kim Seon-gyu, the father-in-law of General Cha Kimoon, served as the 10th Division commander in the late 1960s. His son-in-law, General Cha, also served as the 25th commander of the 37th Division in 1994." In response, General Cha Kimoon said, "I seem to have a special connection with the number 37. My father-in-law served as the commander of the 37th Division, I also served as the commander of the 37th Division, and I am concluding my 37 years of military service at the 37th Division. Today is also my wife's birthday." The guests applauding could easily guess how the general and his wife had met.

Among the sequences of presenting bouquets and souvenirs by peers, classmates, friends, church members, juniors, relatives, and so on, the most striking moment was when the beautifully looking daughter came out with her husband, handed the bouquet to her father's arms, and pressed her lips to her father's cheek with an expression of utmost happiness. The father showed a joyful yet shy expression as expected. How many retirement ceremonies, regardless of the workplace or position, can be this splendid, dignified, and proud? No workplace demands risking one's life. Only the military does. That risk is not for oneself but for the nation and the people. What could be more sacred and honorable than that? The general, who devoted his youth to this sacred profession and is now retiring, puts aside the hardships of facing life-and-death situations, thanks the glory and fortune, and steps out of the military gates with satisfaction. The farewell applause from the soldiers lined up along the over 1 mile road from the command building to the main gate seems to remind us again what true life is.

General! Many generals before us have hung up their uniforms, symbols of honor and glory, only to be caught in various ups and downs, witnessing moments when their sacred honor vanished overnight. Although your uniform has been hung up, we sincerely wish you always live with the same dignity, honor, and respect as you do today.

Kim Gi-bong, Head of the Courier Business Division, Korea Logisties Co., Ltd

Kim Gi-bong, who wrote the above article, is a classmate of the ACAD program at Seoul National University's Graduate School of Public Administration and a person like a close brother with whom I share a deeper friendship than childhood friends. This writing vividly conveys the scene at that time, making it a treasured piece of memory for me.

Cha Jeong-seok, Kim Kyeong-ah, The Author, Cha Soo-jin, Kim Joo-hyeuk

At the time of my retirement, my son Cha Jeong-seok came to see me wearing his ROTC uniform, having just joined the program. The ROTC was very popular among university students, as it helped cultivate leadership through experiences in responsibility, organizational management, and command. Since its establishment in 1961, the ROTC has produced countless officers who have gone on to enter society, forming a major pressure group that now constitutes a significant part of Korea's leadership class. A powerful ROTC network has been formed, far beyond typical senior-junior relationships in universities.

My son, Cha Jeong-seok, was admitted to the ROTC.

ROTC officers who serve long-term receive the same promotions, assignments, and training as graduates of the Korea Military Academy. This system, introduced from the United States, is becoming a global trend in line with advanced nations. In the U.S., ROTC officers now make up the main force of the military, surpassing those from West Point. Among the 17 generals serving with U.S. Forces in Korea, the majority are ROTC graduates, with only one being a graduate of the U.S. Military Academy. The fact that most commanders of U.S. Forces in Korea are ROTC officers shows just how significant the ROTC is in the United States. In Korea, interest in the ROTC also continues to grow, making me all the more proud that Cha Jeong-seok has joined the program.

I gave my encouragement and applause to Cha Jeong-seok's resolute determination to follow in his father's footsteps and become a soldier. I confess I could not properly care for my family during my military service, having devoted my entire life solely to serving the nation and the people. As a result, I inevitably could not give as much attention to my children's education as those in other professions might have.

My family moved on average once every year and a half. Throughout my military career, I moved 25 times. During Cha Jeong-seok elementary school years alone, he attended Cheonbo, Pocheon, Yeongdo, and Yale Elementary School, so it was only natural that he could not receive a stable education. Whenever he started to settle in and adapt to school life, we would move again, and he would have to transfer schools. It felt as though he had no true alma mater, yet at the same time, he had many. Even so, Cha Jeong-seok adapted well to new environments and made friends easily. In high school, he was confidently elected student body president through an open vote, where he demonstrated outstanding leadership within the school.

My daughter-in-law, Park Bok-seon, and my son, Cha Jeong-seok

After being commissioned as an officer and promoted to the rank of captain, Cha Jeong-seok was serving as the commanding officer of the guard unit in Panmunjom when he brought his girlfriend and said he wanted to marry her. She was Captain Park Bok-seon, serving in the Army Intelligence Command. Captain Park had graduated with honors from the Department of Japanese at Kyungbook National University and had been commissioned as a long-term service officer.

While working as a Japanese instructor at the Intelligence School, she was recognized for her abilities and was assigned strategic intelligence duties at the Army Intelligence Command. Hailing from a distinguished family in Ulsan, Captain Park was raised with care and strong values under the guidance of a devoted mother. Throughout her academic career, she consistently received scholarships and completed her university education as an exemplary student.

My wife and I have always prioritized our children's wishes regarding marriage. We believed that if they truly liked and loved each other, there was no need to consider any other conditions.

The wedding of Cha Jeong-seok and Park Bok-seon

This was the case with our daughter Cha Soo-jin, and we chose to do the same for Cha Jeong-seok. After both families met for a formal introduction, the marriage proceeded smoothly and without delay. The wedding ceremony was held at the Army Club in Samgakji, Seoul, and was officiated by Kim Tae-young, the Minister of National Defense.

The wedding ceremony officiated by Minister of National Defense Kim Tae-young

Granddaughter Cha Min-seo, Grandson Cha Min-woo

My first granddaughter, Cha Min-seo, was born. I chose her name, making sure it suited the times, was easy to say, and pleasant to hear. I also considered the generational naming tradition of the Cha family. Shortly after, my grandson Cha Min-woo was born. I was deeply grateful to my daughter-in-law for giving birth to both granddaughter and grandson. She loved the military life and took care of her in-laws as if they were her own family, which made her even more beloved.

Having overcome difficult challenges and grown wisely under the care of her maternal grandmother and grandfather, Cha Soo-jin developed a strong and upright sense of resilience on her own. Cha Jeong-seok, despite transferring schools many times, adapted well to new environments and grew up with clear judgment and a firm life philosophy even in extreme situations. As parents, there is nothing more to be thankful for than seeing our children grow up properly, find good partners, and live well.

Epilogue (The Ten Commandments of Leadership)

Having experienced leadership firsthand throughout a lifetime and lectured on leadership at university, the author cannot overlook conveying the essential virtues of a leader to those who seek eternal life. Summarizing the core of the author's leadership learned through 37 years of selfless service and practical theory, this is presented as the Ten Commandments of Leadership, serving as the conclusion of this book.

Leadership is an academic field that has been continuously discussed and studied since the formation of human society. Excellent leadership is both a skill and an art that exerts influence over members of an organization to move the organization in the direction desired by the leader. True leadership is possible only when voluntary obedience from the members follows, so leaders must relentlessly cultivate their leadership. As ancient wisdom says, the noble person walks "the practice of the great way", meaning a leader must always walk an honorable and confident path. Humans face two paths: emotion and will. One can walk the path of the noble person only by controlling emotions and firmly holding onto one's will. Within a person's heart lurks the instinct to pursue complacent desires. If a person can fight and overcome these primal instincts, they can be considered to have achieved the first stage as a leader. Leadership comes from self-cultivation, which involves not deceiving oneself, loving others, and winning the battle against oneself.

The essence of leadership lies in correctly understanding the group's collective consciousness to achieve the organization's goals and finding measures to address it. Therefore, based on my practical experience, I have summarized the Ten Commandments of Leadership as follows.

1. Have a vision.

If a vision is set, it must be able to be realized concretely. A leader without a vision is not a leader but merely a manager. A manager accepts reality as it is, whereas a leader challenges reality. A manager only sees what is immediately in front of them, but a leader looks far ahead in the long term. A manager focuses on "when" and "how," but a leader questions "what" and "why."

Have you ever heard the term "world-class manager"? However, there is such a thing as a "world-class leader"— political leaders, military leaders, religious leaders, human rights leaders, and so on. They lead. Therefore, to be a leader, a vision is necessary, and the difference between a leader and a manager lies in whether or not they have a vision.

2. Set an example.

Just as the tone is set at the top, leadership's essence lies foremost in setting an example. A leader must always act with the awareness that, like goldfish in a fishbowl, everyone is watching every move, and must show exemplary behavior in all actions. When observing a successful leader's subordinates, one can see how they strive to resemble their leader in every aspect. Listening to their voices on the phone, it is noticeable how similar they are to their superior's tone, and their walking style and mannerisms also mirror those of their leader. Therefore, a leader should cultivate a habit of transparency in life and demonstrate exemplary language and behavior to their team members.

A leader must always manage the organization with a focus on subordinates and maintain an attitude of dedication to them. The leader should sacrifice, devote, and commit fully to the organization to which they belong. Only then will the members develop a sense of ownership and do their best for their group. People naturally want to belong to a good organization. The leader must inherit the honor and tradition of the organization and create an atmosphere where everyone strives to do their best, no matter how small the task.

A leader must earn the respect and trust of the members and inspire them to succeed in their tasks. Trust is gained by strictly adhering to high standards and self-discipline in one's behavior. Shifting responsibility onto subordinates causes a loss of trust. The leader must bear responsibility. Only then will subordinates trust and follow their superiors. If a leader shirks responsibility with an attitude of "You did it, so you take responsibility. I don't care," the situation becomes difficult. The work fails without a chance to solve the problem, and the leader loses the subordinates' respect. Therefore, a leader can earn trust and respect only by leading by example and setting a model for their juniors.

3. Keep emotional balance.

A leader must never lose their temper. Anger is the enemy of leadership. A leader should respect the values of their members and inspire motivation, not discourage them by showing anger. Cry inside but smile outside. Emotions must be controlled internally. Do not show your joy outwardly. The foolish laugh loudly, but the wise laugh quietly to themselves. Do not get angry just because someone has not done something perfectly. Everyone has different personalities and values. People have strengths and weaknesses; some supervisors see weaknesses as positives, while others see strengths as flaws.

Do not express dissatisfaction when your opinion is not accepted. Showing dissatisfaction is a sign of immaturity. A leader must have patience and self-discipline and think carefully before speaking or acting. As the Talmud says, "Words are your servant, but once they leave your mouth, they become your master." Speak cautiously and avoid speaking impulsively based on emotion.

After the Korean War, as the military expanded, young generals lacking knowledge and experience were promoted to high positions but still successfully led their units. This was because they minimized speech and established authority through silence. For example, when a staff officer came for approval, if the general did not understand the content well, he would nod, and if displeased, shake his head side to side—thus successfully commanding through silence.

There are many cases where leaders regret using emotional language when they should have shown patience. Leaders often hurt subordinates and cause stress by speaking thoughtlessly without considering the impact. Sometimes, this breaks subordinates' morale and reduces work efficiency. Conflicts within the organization often stem from a leader's lack of patience.

Once, after finishing a meeting, I could not find a driver to take me back to the unit. Upon hearing no driver was available, I called the unit and lost my temper over an unimportant matter, creating a tense atmosphere in the unit. Early in my career as a junior commander, I mistakenly thought that showing anger was necessary to establish authority and ensure quick obedience.

One must not confuse losing one's temper with giving constructive criticism. Surprisingly, many leaders shout angrily or curse. Even without cursing, yelling only breeds resentment and is of no help. Leaders must not act or speak based on emotion but should lead with thoughtful consideration while maintaining emotional balance. Only then will members respect the leader and follow willingly.

4. Know your team members and use them according to their abilities.

It is extremely important to understand organization members and give the impression that you know them deeply. When you learn subordinates' names, family details, and hometowns and use this information during direct conversations, subordinates will surprisingly respect their superior and become loyal, assured that they are genuinely cared for. When commanding subordinates, tasks should be assigned according to their abilities. Forcing a recruit with less than 100 days of service to march 100 kilometers or demanding capabilities that only veterans possess will cause problems and ultimately lead to ruin.

Reprimands should be given while leaving an escape route. If an excuse is given, pretend not to notice and let it pass. If someone is at a loss, offer comfort. Teach them if a task was not done properly due to a lack of knowledge. When a person feels trapped with no way out, they may act unpredictably, even violently or self-destructively. Sharing your past failures is also a method: "If only I had done this or that back then... I regret it now..." Avoid comparing people to others. Saying things like "Manager Kim is your peer! Go learn from him!" or "Manager Kim does well, so why don't you?" only deeply wounds pride. Do not just point out faults; kindly guide them to do the work properly.

Criticize the wrong actions themselves. Comments attacking personality or character hurt pride, causing resentment and discouragement, resulting in the opposite effect. Saying things like "How did you become a section chief after doing this?" "Quit immediately!" or "Do you even know what this official document is?" only creates problems. Instead, point out specifics clearly: "This part is a bit unclear. How about correcting it this way?" This encourages subordinates to recognize mistakes, take responsibility, and courageously handle tasks.

When corruption occurs, do not hesitate to say clearly, "I am hearing these things, so be careful not to let me hear them again." If corruption persists, decisive action must be taken. Remember that organizational efficiency improves when subordinates are well understood and tasks are assigned according to their abilities. Know your subordinates and use them according to their abilities.

5. Do not show your weaknesses to your team members.

There is a story about an elementary school student who was greatly disappointed after seeing their respected teacher enter the restroom. When people see weaknesses in a superior they respect and want to follow, they become deeply disappointed. Therefore, a leader should highlight their strengths and minimize their weaknesses. It is said that Napoleon always wore high-heeled shoes to hide his short stature. A leader must pay special attention to avoid disappointing the organization members who follow them.

6. Give orders through the organizational chain and apply rewards and punishments accordingly.

A leader must not ignore the organization or give orders carelessly. If it is unavoidable to provide instructions directly to a subordinate's subordinate, the fact of that instruction should later be communicated to the immediate subordinate. Only then can trust be built between superior and subordinate, minimizing adverse effects on the organization's chain of command. Even if a department head must give orders directly to a section chief, informing the division chief afterward will strengthen trust between the department head and the division chief and prevent unnecessary misunderstandings.

Rewards and punishments must be administered appropriately. Those who perform well should be rewarded, and those who do not should be punished. Praise subordinates before many people, but hold them accountable and reprimand them discreetly. In other words, it is best to praise where others can see, but criticize in private. Public criticism can hurt pride, cause loss of composure, and provoke resistance rather than reflection.

7. Develop yourself and let go of greed.

No one is perfect. Leaders, too, have their shortcomings.

Therefore, a leader must engage in self-reflection and self-discipline before leading subordinates and developing aides. Without properly refining oneself, it is impossible to guide subordinates correctly. Developing oneself requires more effort than others. Spending an extra hour every day, more actively than others, for ten years amounts to 3,650 hours of additional effort and results.

As William James said, "Change your thoughts and you change your behavior; change your behavior and you change your habits; change your habits and you change your character; change your character and you change your destiny." A leader must continually cultivate correct thinking and behavior to foster personal qualities and abilities. A leader must develop the power of self-mastery to build morality, character, ethics, and wisdom. Self-mastery is the ability to fight and overcome oneself, which is not easily achieved. Humans naturally seek comfort and pleasure and are constantly challenged by various temptations. Overcoming these internal enemies with self-mastery is the shortcut to cultivating a leader's way.

To be strong is to be free of greed. Let go of greed. In Go, many games are lost by being greedy in a very advantageous position. In golf, trying too hard to increase the driving distance often causes a OB shot. As the Bible says, "Blessed are the poor in spirit, for theirs is the kingdom of heaven; blessed are the pure in heart, for they shall see God." Letting go of greed brings peace of mind and composure. "Always rejoice and give thanks in all circumstances." The conditions given are the same for everyone. How one thinks about and overcomes their given environment determines their happiness.

In Eumseong, Chungcheongbuk-do, there is a place called Flower Village. About 2,000 abandoned people live there, including alcoholics, mentally ill patients, the physically and mentally disabled, and tuberculosis patients—people who have no strength left to survive in this world. Yet their faces shine with happiness. No matter how difficult the circumstances, if one takes them as opportunities, gives thanks, and overcomes crises, they can become a victor in life, and their character will deepen. A leader must make continuous efforts to cultivate self-discipline with the power of self-mastery and a grateful heart, beginning with oneself.

8. Be willing to change.

In response to the changing times and ongoing reforms, it is essential to embrace transformation with the mindset of "being a better version of yourself every day." Modern society is evolving with each passing day. The progress of civilization from the 5th century BC to the Industrial Revolution in the 20th century carries roughly the same weight as the changes that occurred in just the 100 years following the Industrial Revolution. Since then, the pace has only accelerated, and today, a single year brings more change than what used to take a decade in the past.

As the Talmud says, "If you are not expanding your knowledge, you are regressing." Standing still means becoming a dropout in terms of knowledge. One of the primary ways to cultivate knowledge is through reading, which provides indirect experience. Regrettably, Koreans' reading lags behind that of other countries. The average annual reading volume for Americans is 10.8 books; for Japanese, it is 12.7, whereas for Koreans, it is only 2.7. Leaders must make reading a habit and steadily strive to enhance their knowledge. Reading at least one book per week is essential so that by pursuing change through knowledge, leaders can equip themselves with the qualities of a desirable leader.

9. Put aside personal interests and act fairly and justly.

One must have the spirit of "to sacrifice oneself for the greater good of the nation," abandoning personal desires to devote one's life entirely to the country, the nation, and humanity. When a leader becomes entangled in personal matters and seeks the welfare and benefits of themselves and their close circle, they lose their qualification as a leader. Such leaders cause the atmosphere of their organization to decline toward stagnation.

When new leaders assume office, they begin by scrutinizing questions like "Where is his hometown?" "What is his background?" "Who are he close to?" This leads to a culture where some people "succeed" and others "fail." Using connections extending even to friends of friends, factions with impure motives form. Furthermore, actions that influence personnel and command for personal gain may cause the organization to collapse.

Therefore, a leader must never attend private gatherings with exclusive elements obstructing official command functions. If such groups with impure motives exist, they must immediately disband to establish leadership. A leader can maintain their position only by abandoning personal interests and acting with fairness and integrity.

10. Maintain strong physical health and be a leader who puts principles into practice.

No matter how excellent one's character and professional knowledge may be, one cannot become a capable leader without good health. Leaders must always do their best to maintain their health through a regular lifestyle. To keep healthy, I jogged every morning. Waking up early, breathing fresh air while jogging, and then taking a shower afterward improves work efficiency and makes the body feel light, filling the day with joy. Along with health management, pursuing hobbies is also a good method. Using leisure time to play tennis, table tennis, horseback riding, hiking, skiing, or badminton helps maintain health and develop one's hobbies.

A leader without action is not a leader. There is a saying: "Planning 5%, execution 95%." This means that execution is more important than planning. No matter how good the plan is, without execution, it is just an unreachable dream. Execution lies in doing one's best and not being afraid of failure. The happiest time for a person is when they do their utmost in the assigned task and believe that even if they were to do it again, they could not do better.

When anyone is first given a task, they feel burdened and fearful of the outcome. However, as the saying goes, "With focused spirit, nothing is impossible." If one puts one's whole heart and energy into something, nothing is impossible. Therefore, evaluating things with a positive and proactive mindset and approaching the task with a "Can Do" attitude will lead to enthusiastic work and positive results.

When carrying out a task, one must carefully deliberate, make accurate judgments, and prepare thorough plans. Once the preparation is perfect, bold execution is necessary. One must be obsessed with accomplishing the task. "Without obsessive passion, there is no greatness." After completing the task, a detailed analysis should be made to enable improved performance in the future. After dedicating full effort to complete the work, one must adopt the attitude of entrusting the result to fate.

In conclusion, a leader must have a vision and lead by

example. He should not openly show emotions but maintain a poker face. He must understand his subordinates well and assign tasks according to their abilities.

He should not reveal his weaknesses and must practice fair reward and punishment. He should avoid actions that destroy the system, continuously strive for self-improvement, and give up personal greed. Creativity, developing something new, and conducting oneself fairly and with integrity are essential. Above all, strong physical health is crucial. Without stamina, one lacks the qualifications of a leader. A leader must practice with strong stamina. Theory without practice is just an illusion.